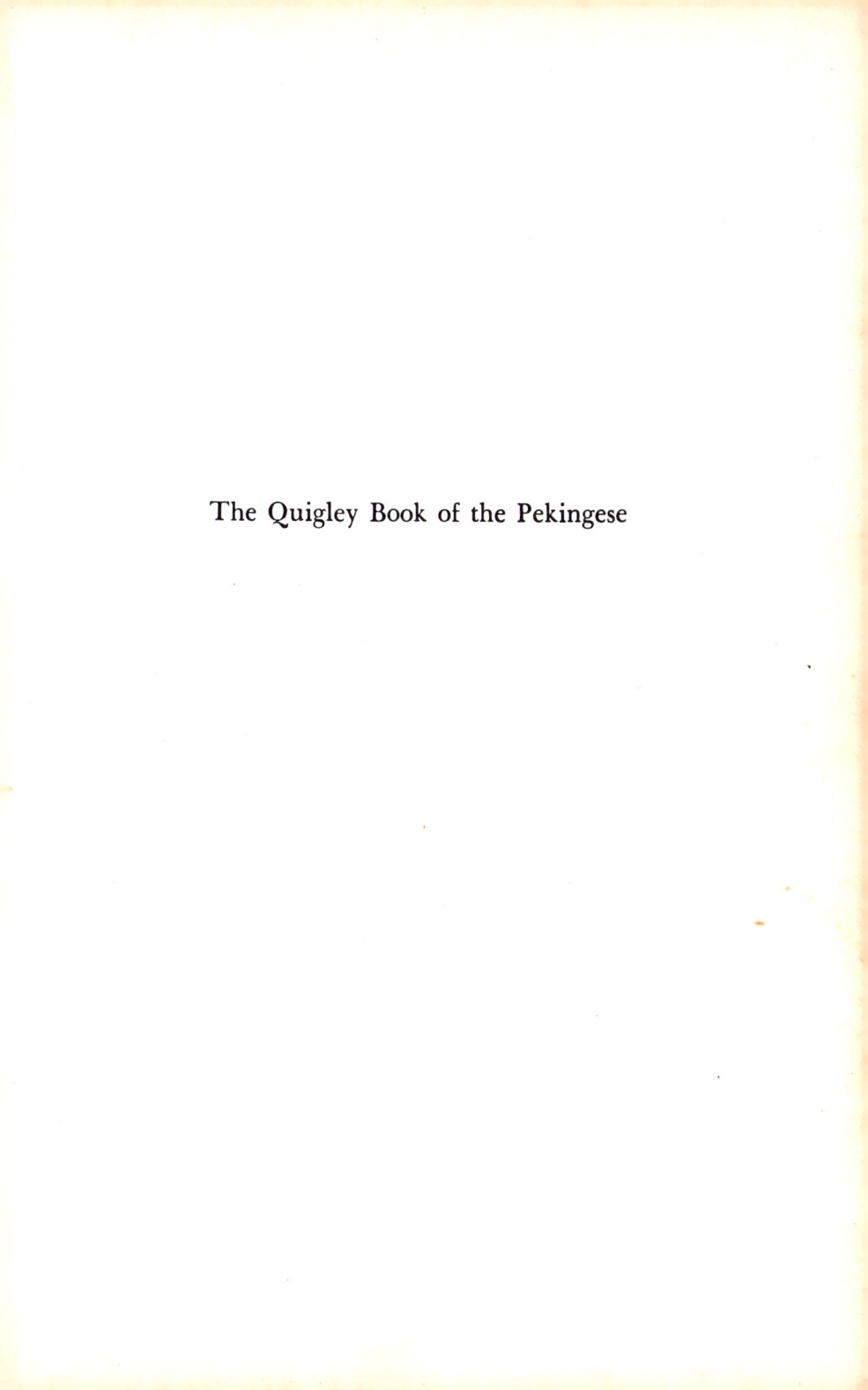

The Quigley Book of the Pekingese

THE QUIGLEY BOOK
OF THE Pekingese

By *DOROTHY QUIGLEY*

1964

HOWELL BOOK HOUSE

845 THIRD AVENUE

NEW YORK, N.Y. / 10022

Ch. Bonraye Fu Toi of Orchard Hill with breeder-owner, Mrs. Quigley.

Copyright © by Howell Book House Inc.

Library of Congress Catalog Card Number: 64–25227

No part of this book may be reproduced without permission in writing from the publisher.
Printed in U.S.A.

In Memory
of
Ch. Jai Son Fu the Golden Fleece

*"So we know from Mount Olympus,
do not hunt the Golden Fleece,
we have it here."*

Contents

	Preface	
1	The Pekingese Mirror or How It All Began	7
2	Origin and History	11
3	Character	18
4	Pekingese Past and Present	27
5	Mistakes and Successes	88
6	Care of the Bred Bitch	98
7	Whelping	107
8	The Matron and Her Nestlings	116
9	Care of Young Puppies	125
10	Feeding the Grown Dog	135
11	Diseases and Nursing	144
12	Grooming for Home and Show Ring	155
13	Colors and Color Breeding	162
14	Judging the Pekingese	171
15	Traveling by Car	176
16	Shipping by Rail and Air	180
17	Epilogue	187

Preface

Having lived most of my life with Pekingese, I cannot write of them as just dogs since to me they are more than that. They are characters, each one a distinct personality, each with individual faults or virtues, as the case may be, exactly as one finds such differences in the human family. In fact, as all who have raised them know, Pekingese are more like human beings than any breed in existence.

We have raised many intelligent dogs, Dobermans and hunting dogs, but in the many years of our experience with various breeds, I consider that no other dog has as much to offer in companionship, devotion, and intelligence as the Pekingese. Being small, he can travel anywhere, under one's arm or in a case, or he can walk gaily on a lead. Being the most characteristically quiet of all toy dogs, he is not given to yapping and thus to disturbing the neighbors.

To further my contention that the Pekingese is more human-like than other dogs, let us go back to ancient Chinese history to understand his quite unique origin and mode of life. Before doing this, however, I believe that the story of my experience with our first small dog will prove of interest to the owner of a house pet as well as to the novice who plans to raise Pekingese.

The Pekingese Mirror—Here's Looking at You! Ch. Tulo of Alderbourne of Orchard Hill as a puppy.

1

The Pekingese Mirror or How It All Began

EVERYTHING in this house is old now, "antique," including ourselves! We started our antique collection in 1924 when Orchard Hill was built, and we concentrated on American Chippendale furniture and other Americana. Shortly thereafter, and purely by accident, Pekingese became an added hobby. Here is how it began. . . .

In the early 1920's I would have placed Pekingese way down on the long list of dogs for which I had either liking or real respect. I had always thought of them as lap dogs suitable only for old ladies and city apartments; as needing silk cushions, neck bows and special coddling. How fortunate it is that so often fate barges in and radically changes our opinions for us! How little I knew that the time would come when, having learned to know Pekingese, I would regard them as the most desirable of all the many dogs in the world.

My daughter was in school in Paris, and when we went over to bring her home for her summer vacation, to our horror we found she had bought from a pet shop a Pekingese which she insisted on keeping because she adored him. His manners were exemplary. She had trained him to lead, to sit up, to stay quietly where put. What a name she had given him—Golubchik!—at the suggestion of a White Russian family living in Paris whom she had visited. Golubchik means "My Little Love."

We live in the country in one of Pennsylvania's great game sections which in those days abounded in native grouse. So of course we raised hunting dogs, mainly English Setters, Pointers and a few Beagles. No one, I think, can blame us for being not a little apprehensive as to the way a Pekingese would fit into such a menage. We need not have worried for nothing whatsoever phased the redoubtable Golubchik.

He was a purebred, but no pedigree came with him, so all he had to offer was personality and an ideal temperament. In short order, he not only won our hearts completely, he owned the place! At first the hunting dogs were jealous of him but they too soon fell under his spell and before the month was out Golubchik became head man and ran us all.

We have about 248 acres, woods and fields, and regardless of the threat of Spanish needles and cockleburrs, every morning when Golubchik was put out for exercise he teamed up with the Beagles. Away they went chasing rabbits, and to hear his yip-yip punctuating the baying of the hounds was something I can never forget. He would return of course full of burrs, panting and apologetic; take his scolding as he endured the pain of untangling those burrs; promised not to do it again, or so it seemed to us. Then, at the very first opportunity he would take to the fields once more. This six pounds of tireless energy, this tiny lion dog afraid of nothing could follow a Setter or a Beagle for hours.

To Canada we took him on our yearly fishing trips, and to Northern Quebec. How patiently he sat in the boat watching us catch trout, but with what a bored expression that tried to tell us he would rather leave the boat and trail us through the woods. Not that Golubchik did not like trout exactly, for he did, but mainly as something very good to eat.

The Pekingese is anything but a lap dog; he belongs in the country although he adapts himself as well to the apartment. As a *dog*, he has every quality anyone might desire. He is quiet, affectionate, fearless, and more easily cared for than most breeds.

All this and more we learned as we loved and enjoyed little

Golubchik for two full years, and when he was accidentally killed we grieved as over the loss of our best friend. He taught us all we knew of the ideal temperament, of loyalty, dignity and obedience, and above all else of the generous response that typifies Pekingese character. Golubchik died before his time, but our love and admiration for his kind could not die, and so we decided he must be replaced by another of the same breed.

Golubchik left no progeny, but so indelibly was he written into our hearts that the ideal of his character and temperament actually became the foundation of the Orchard Hill Pekingese Kennels.

During Golubchik's all too short life we learned little enough about Pekingese as a breed. It was as a dog, a vivid personality, that he attracted and held us to such an extent we could not seem to let him go; so we decided to have some of this same kind, to raise them, to establish a Pekingese kennel.

True to the tenets of the uninitiated the world over, we answered the most glamorous advertisement, "the Largest and Best Kennel of Pekingese." We did not question; we wanted the best and this ad said the best! By mail, that is, sight unseen, we purchased a bitch puppy with the understanding that we could call for her. Upon arrival we found three in the litter on display and the clever saleswoman persuaded us to take the lot, Sister, Brownie, and Blackie.

We knew nothing about the breed's best physical characteristics; we had never read the standard. Hence, it meant little, if anything, that Brownie had a dudley nose, that Blackie was utterly unsuitable as a sire, and that Sister was worth perhaps twenty-five dollars as a pet rather than the $200.00 we paid, plus as much more for each of her brothers. They were cute and attractive and we were confident that we had chosen well. I was actually proud of my purchases and like all novices, I decided to exhibit them without delay. I entered them in every possible classification, but to my embarrassment, each won a first ribbon only when alone in the class, or a fourth if four were shown.

Patiently the judge told me where my dogs failed, and at his suggestion I wrote to the president of the Pekingese Club telling her I was interested in raising Pekingese. Through addresses which she sent me, I got in touch with a reliable breeder and through her imported my first good dogs, Ch. Grey Spider and Int. Ch. Sandee of Hesketh. Then I brought over all the Sutherland Av. dogs, twelve of them, from the late Frances Mary Weaver, who due to failing health was forced to give up her famous kennel.

Brownie, Blackie and Sister were given away as pets, but they proved a good investment, since through them we acquired one of the most beautiful and most valuable antique mirrors in this country! The elderly woman from whom we bought the three dogs lived in an old house on Long Island, with her kennel in the rear. Being polite, and I presume not wanting us to see her other dogs, she displayed the three puppies for us in the parlor!

The parlor was usually kept closed, but it was opened up for our visit and there, over the puppy pen, hung the mirror! After we had paid for the dogs, I asked her if any of her old furniture was for sale. She replied, "Yes, anything I have is for sale." I said, "How about that mirror?" We had paid $200.00 each for the dogs and I suppose that price was foremost in her mind, so she replied, "Two hundred dollars for the mirror."

"Isn't that rather high?" I countered. "I see the flowers at the top of the cartouche spray are missing."

To my amazement she said quickly, "Oh no, they are up in the attic!"

We finally departed with three Pekingese, those give-away pets, but we also had a priceless American Chippendale mirror. This rare mirror, in its original condition, was later appraised by a noted authority on American furniture, and we were offered three times what the mirror and the dogs had cost us. It is one of our finest antiques and a constant reminder of those early days and our first dogs. It is appropriately and affectionately called "The Pekingese Mirror."

2
Origin and History

Having decided to raise Pekingese, I purchased several English books on the subject and found the breed's Chinese origin a fascinating tale. I realized why Golubchik had won our hearts. Centuries of adoration and special care back of him had made him the irresistible little creature we had loved and lost.

His astonishing history goes back to the coming of Buddha and to the conversion of all China to Buddhism. This event, which changed the course of Eastern history, changed also the status of the little Chinese dog now known as the Pekingese. The symbol of the new religion brought from India was the lion, that most dreaded of wild beasts which from the religious viewpoint personified human wickedness. Tamed and conquered by the holiness of Buddha, the lion thereafter became Buddha's faithful servant. When the Chinese were converted to Buddhism they too adopted the lion as its symbol, hence the lion came to be the most common figure in their art as well as in their religion.

However, there were no lions in China as in India, and the few specimens sent to the Emperor did not survive, consequently there was no living symbol of Buddha's greatness until someone discovered that the King of Beasts resembled the Emperor's dog of Fu. These dogs had various names—palace dogs, temple dogs, and dogs of Fu

Rare carved Ivory Fu dogs depicting their evolution from past to present. Given to me by the British Pekingese Club.

Pair of rare carved teakwood Fu dogs. Note puppy under figure, also paw holding down the Earth. (Quigley collection.)

Rare bronze incense burner inlaid with cloisonné showing Temple scenes. Fu dog on top with paw holding down the Earth. Handles are studded with semi-precious stones.

Rare carved ivory Kylin. Chinese conception of the earliest Fu dog. Loose ball in mouth that rolls around represents the Earth.

or guard dogs, and now the lion dog. From then on, the lion dog became the living model in art and religion; and the Lord Buddha is depicted with his sacred lion dog, the dog of Fu, ancient ancestor of our Pekingese. The real lion faded from the picture, and the lion dog began a career of glory lasting many centuries, in fact, until the tragic downfall of the Empire.

These special dogs were reared as semi-sacred, and in those early days those which most closely resembled the lion were kept in the Temple in charge of the high priests. The fiercer, more lion-like dogs came from the Province of Kylin and were noted for extreme grotesqueness of type and fierce grin. Today we often describe a good muzzle as a wide Kylin mouth. The smaller, daintier dogs were kept by the Emperor and as favorite house dogs were given highest mandarin rank. Created princes and dukes, they were granted court revenues. Eunuchs and officers of state paid them homage while Imperial guards kept watch and personal servants attended to their needs. They were exercised in ceremonial fashion or carried in sumptuous palanquins. They were bathed with rare perfumes and as the constant companions of the Emperor and the ladies of the court they were petted and regarded as holy charges. The very tiny ones, the highly prized "sleeve dogs," were carried about in the voluminous sleeves of the robes worn by both men and women at court. They accepted as their just due this exaggerated respect and learned to play their various roles in the elaborate court ceremonies. Adorned with ribbons and bells they lead court processions while others held the Emperor's train in their teeth.

Stringent regulations prohibited the removal of these dogs from the palace, and terrible punishments were meted out to those who attempted to steal them. For such a crime death by stoning was merciful as compared with the usual Chinese torture of "death by ten thousand slices." Not until 1905 did the Dowager Empress abolish this frightful punishment.

The Imperial puppies, like the Imperial babies, were put out to nurse; they were given to foster mothers, the waiting women of the court, in place of their own infant girls, these unwanted human babies being drowned or otherwise disposed of. Reared like children, the dogs became almost human, and this characteristic has persisted down through the ages. All this luxury, this exaggerated homage, strangely, did not spoil the temperament of the little lion

Silver Chinese warrior, inlaid with semi-precious stones. Note Fu dog design on chest armor. (Quigley col.)

Huge bronze Kylin guarding Imperial Palace Throne Room. Mrs. Alix Lambert of Cheltenham, England, kindly sent me this picture. It stands on carved white marble plinth. Mrs. Lambert, standing in the foreground, gives us an idea of the great size. This interesting picture was taken before World War II when she was visiting in Peking.

dogs. They remained highly intelligent and loyal; they were intrepid fighters and like their counterpart the lion would fight to the death if provoked.

The actual origin of the dog of Fu, the Pekingese as a dog, may always remain something of a mystery. Chinese historians, however, tell us that it has existed as long as the Empire itself, unchanged in 4000 years! Quaint legends tell of the love of the lion for the marmoset; how the lion prayed to Buddha to make him small enough in stature to find favor with his lady, but begging that he might retain his great heart so as to love her more. The legend goes on to say that the lord Buddha changed the lion into the lion dog, leaving him his great heart and his courage. This version I like to believe since it describes in fairy-tale fashion what we want in Pekingese today.

Some accounts claim that breeding for type was not begun until the Tang Dynasty in the 17th Century or thereabouts. The term Peking Dog—Peiching Kou—was not used until hundreds of years later when the capital under the Manchus was moved to Peking. It was under the Manchus that the Peking Palace dogs reached their height of glory. Other sources tell that the shaggy, small terrier of Tibet was brought to China and used with the lion dog to increase coat and mane. In any event those breeding plans of long ago were successful. From the better coated, shaggy Tibetan Ha Po and the grotesque little dogs of Fu evolved the mane and ruff, the fringes and the longer plume for the tail. Very early Chinese pictures of Pekingese did not depict the full coat and the long tail that resulted from this selective breeding. But for hundreds of years with true Chinese love of the grotesque, the dogs were bred for flatness of face, low bowed legs and small size. Yet with due oriental concern for symmetry and balanced structure, they made the Pekingese type and standard of today. His close contact with people gave him an intimate knowledge of human nature. His adoring slaves were to be treated as such, but members of the royal court were to be charmed and amused by his winsome antics. These things tended to develop the Pekingese temperament as it is, a combination of little dictator or merry jester.

Moreover, the name Pekingese was not used for these dogs until they were fairly well known in England, and after the Pekin Palace Dog Association was formed and their first show held in 1907.

Following the Boxer uprising, and after the sacking of the Summer Palace, a few specimens were brought to England from Pekin. While looting, the Palace soldiers found four little dogs in the apartment of the Emperor's aunt; she had committed suicide when the troops entered the grounds, and her faithful dogs were found guarding her body. The smallest of the four was later presented to England's Queen Victoria by General Dunn upon his return to London. Appropriately named "Lootie," she lived for ten years at Windsor Castle where she had her picture painted by the great Landseer. The other Pekin dogs became the property of the Duchess of Richmond and Admiral Lord John Hay. Not many years later Mr. and Mrs. Douglas Murray brought home a few more, two of these being the well known Ah Cum and Mimosa which now head Pekingese genealogical charts. From these dogs, then called Pekingese Spaniels, have descended today's modern Pekingese.

But to Mrs. Loftus Allen we owe the introduction of the breed to the public when she exhibited her Pekin Peter in London in 1894. This was the first Pekingese ever entered in a dog show. In 1898 the Kennel Club, England, recognized the breed, giving it the official name Pekingese.

A few Palace dogs, gifts or loot as the case may be, came to America shortly after their introduction into England. Miss Carl, the American artist who had painted the Dowager Empress' favorite little dog, "Tzu Hsi," had received a particolor puppy as a present. The Empress also gave one of her Palace dogs to Alice Roosevelt when she and her father, President Theodore Roosevelt, visited Peking shortly before the death of the Empress. Mr. J. P. Morgan, Sr., too, who visited Peking about this time, admired the dogs and brought a pair home with him. Incidentally, Mr. Morgan, years later, while looking over the dogs in the Alderbourne Kennels, near London, saw Ch. Yu Chuan of Alderbourne and offered Mrs. Ashton-Cross a fabulous price for him . . . a price I hesitate to name. This was told to me by Marjorie Ashton-Cross herself, who was visiting me at Orchard Hill at the time. Several weeks later her mother cabled that Ch. Yu Chuan had died suddenly from a heart attack. His epigraph should read "Here lies a beloved dog that no money could buy." Yu Chuan was as near perfection as one could breed; his tragic death while so young was mourned by all who knew him. I was indeed fortunate to have owned his wonderful son, Ch. Sutherland Av Hanshih, my first great show dog.

The Chinese-bred dogs of those early days that were brought to this country never had progeny; or the few they may have had soon merged with the English dogs then being imported. We have just one record of a Chinese-born dog gaining show honors in America. A Pekingese was first exhibited here in 1901 in Philadelphia in the miscellaneous class; named Pekin, he belonged to Mrs. George Thomas.

Slowly the Pekingese gained in popularity, and in 1906 was recognized as a breed by the American Kennel Club and granted classes at shows. In 1907, the first male won a championship in America, T'sang of Downshire, owned by Mrs. Morris Mandy. The following year the first female to become a champion had this interesting catalogue entry: Ch. Chaou Ching Ur, born September 12, 1902. Breeder, Dowager Empress of China. Owner, Dr. Mary Cotton.

In April, 1909, the Pekingese Club of America was founded with Mrs. Morris Mandy as President; J. P. Morgan, Sr. was honorary president; Mrs. Benjamin Guinness, Mrs. R. P. McGraun and Dr. Mary Cotton, vice-presidents; and Mrs. M. E. Harby, secretary-treasurer.

The club's initial specialty show was held January 18, 1911 with an entry of ninety-five dogs. It was indeed a fashionable affair with the ballroom of New York's Plaza Hotel suitably decorated with Chinese silks and bronze Fu dogs. Expensive silver trophies were presented to the winners and the show was a great success. Many well-known social leaders attended, some as exhibitors; among them Elbridge Gerry Snow and J. P. Morgan. The future of the Pekingese, and the breed's permanent place in the world of dogs were assured.

3
Character

From the moment we get to know a dog and love him for his responsiveness, his funny little ways, for the thousand and one endearing habits he acquires in the course of his daily life, the question of his appearance begins to mean less and less. Rarely do we think of him as belonging to a certain breed, as being a winner or an also-ran. Affection has transformed him into a little person, loved for himself alone. His character, the spirit of his innermost self is thenceforth the tie that binds. That is why a person can learn to love almost any kind of dog.

At the same time, there is a catch to the old axiom that 'any kind of dog will satisfy the true dog lover.' Not every dog can fit every need. The all-purpose dog is extremely rare if not actually non-existent. We read about him, we hear about him, but I myself have never encountered one, and I know of no one who has.

Size, strength, build, heritage, all combine to make dogs different, and because of their differences some can do things which others cannot. Some excel where others fail. It must be so, else nature would not have provided so many kinds of dogs equipped for so wide a variety of living. The person accustomed to dogs knows this and selects his dog for his natural endowments. He picks the gundog for hunting, the guard dog for courage, the toy dog for companionship.

Ch. Sutherland Av Hanshih, the Fearless One.

Ch. Pier Simba in his antique doll bed with bureau.

Followed too closely, however, this theoretical blueprint is no infallible guide. For, though in the main dogs follow the trade of their forebears, some acquire an astounding versatility, jumping the barrier of heritage to become dogs of assorted accomplishments. You cannot gauge a dog's versatility by looking at him; you discover it only by living with him.

That is what actually happened in my own case. Looking at the Pekingese I thought him a beautiful pet, good for cuddling, but not for much else. Living with him made all the difference; it proved to me that the breed is versatile away and above the average observer's superficial estimate. In other words, he delights to engage in activities which the toy-dog enthusiast has long considered as beyond the strength and capability of one so tiny.

As far as the Pekingese is concerned, small size is solely a matter of measurement, having nothing to do with sturdiness, gameness, endurance or pluck. The Peke is utterly fearless although not aggressive. It is rare indeed for a Pekingese to pick a fight with another dog, but if a Boxer for instance presumed to pick on *him*, he would as likely sail head-on into the Boxer as into the teeth of any other dog large or small which dared accost him. Proud he seems to be of his ancient family lineage, and he looks the part with supercilious eye and sometimes quite a sneer which means 'You keep your distance and I'll keep mine.'

Characteristic Pekingese fearlessness comes to light in a variety of situations, not the least of which I have found to be an almost total disregard of the elements. This in itself is noteworthy for I have seen larger dogs, brave enough under gunfire, reduced to abject fear by the noise of thunder.

Years ago when exhibiting Ch. Sutherland Av Hanshih at an upstate New York show under tents, a terrific storm broke accompanied by thunder, lightning and torrential rains. The few spectators who dared remain for the finals were marooned by the downpour up in the dogs' stalls. The contest for Best in Show had narrowed down to Hanshih and a Scottie, the latter so terrified that his handler had to hold him up literally by the tail. The two dogs were posed on the block, the Scottie shivering with fright, I myself quaking at each thunderclap. There stood Hanshih calm and collected, upright on a loose lead, his tail up and over. If any dog in all the world deserved a Best in Show, that show was Hanshih's! But the Scottie won.

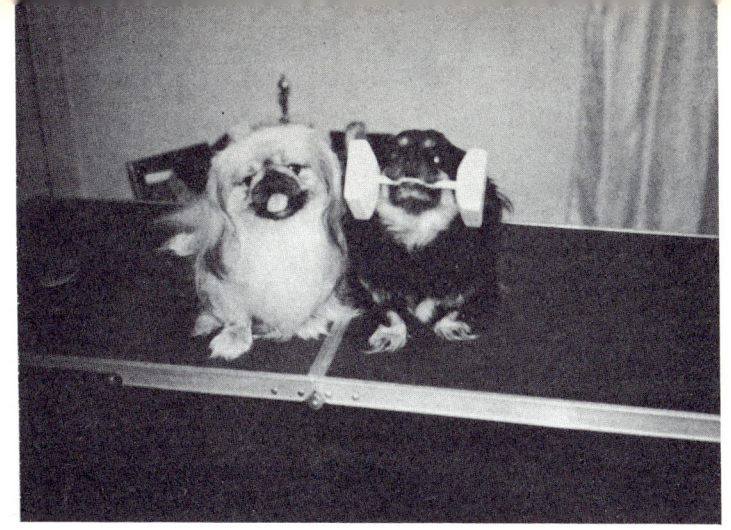

Obedience winners, owned by Otto Harrup and Kerry Allen.

Ch. Fei Jai Yin, another fearless miniature with owner, Mrs. Betty Johnstonbaugh, who has so successfully managed Orchard Hill Kennels.

Even had the two dogs been equal in quality, the Pekingese should have been given the award on temperament alone, for the Scottie from fear lost his Terrier character whereas the Peke in all that tumult posed bold as a lion. This incident I mention as showing a well known characteristic of the breed. The Peke can rise to any occasion; he is seldom flustered by the unexpected; he has courage and to spare. I think that is one of the many reasons why those who own a Pekingese are never thereafter satisfied with a dog of any other kind. Courage is something in man and dog that all of us admire.

What we do not admire oftentimes is stubbornness, and this the average Pekingese has to a marked degree. But stubbornness has its good side when considered in the light of determination. In time of sickness it enables the Peke to put his best foot foremost, to fight to the last ditch for his own survival. The Pekingese possesses the will to live, and live he does frequently through sheer grit and ability to endure suffering, come what may. He never gives up. In distemper this is a most valuable aid, and in the crises of whelping it is priceless.

Stubbornness during training has been decried as a Pekingese fault. Actually I have found it to be a sign of intelligence in the dog coupled with ignorant handling by the trainer. The Pekingese pupil bides his time until he understands the command given and, once he does understand, he interprets correctly and acts in accordance.

Then why, the reader must certainly ask himself, if the Peke can be trained successfully, are there not more obedience-titled dogs in the breed? First, because comparatively few people understand Pekingese temperament sufficiently well to realize the dog's trainability. The moment that is understood and due allowance made for it, this dog cooperates fully with the trainer in whom he has confidence. Second, because the jump demand of open-class obedience procedure appears like an insurmountable hurdle for a dog not built by nature for extended jumping. The fact that the C.D.X. (Companion Dog Excellent) title has been won by Pekingese proves that the dog can transcend his natural build. Nevertheless, jumping is not a recommended form of activity for the average Peke although it is an easily acquired form of fun for dogs fortunate enough to live a life of freedom on the varied terrain of woods and fields.

What a pity our progressively better obedience trial demands could not include at least one either/or provision, that is, a substituted type of proficiency for the jump suited to the excessively short-legged breeds.

One has only to watch a Peke intently to see that he is no lap dog, but a real companion at home anywhere in the world and under any circumstances. Small though he may be, he is a toughy in every sense of the word. Take him with you to the shore and turn him loose on the beach where he runs with the greatest of ease and in speed outstrips most dogs of comparable stride. Take him with you to the lake where he soon learns to swim short distances and to retrieve from the water. Take him to the woods and the hills and watch his spaniel origin assert itself. Given a chance to use it, he has a good nose and will run a rabbit before you know it. All of these things the free-running Peke can do and will do with great enjoyment and no little proficiency.

If perforce his must be the leash-life of restricted spaces, that type of exercise also he will enjoy and with it be content. A commendable ingredient of his makeup is the fact that he is not restive and forever aiming for something he cannot have. With the owner to whom he gives the wealth of his affection he is satisfied to live in one room or in many, in hotel or apartment, in cottage or castle, and he fits equally well in any of these places because his size as well as his temperament so adapts him.

But he must be given enough exercise which no dog, sleeve or outsize, can long do without. If he lives in small quarters, especially will he need at least two leash walks daily. Being small, he does not require the five or ten-mile hike of the large dog, but will get along very well with a mile or two in the park. And if gradually accustomed to it, he benefits from a three to five-mile jaunt in the country.

Now these recommended distances I realize are far apart, and the energy required for each substantially differing. Why do we suggest a mile for the leash walk and three miles for the country jaunt! Simply because the leash walk entails a steady, energy-consuming pep-peg, whereas the country jaunt usually allowed off leash entails frequent little rest periods as well as a change of gait at intervals which the free-running dog instinctively employs to conserve energy and to minimize muscular fatigue.

But one thing should always be kept in mind. Safe exercise distance is slowly progressive, that is, the walk or run at first is fairly short, then increased a trifle each day until the sensibly allowable maximum is reached. Otherwise, strain and exhaustion will be risked where only stimulation is to be desired.

Size considered, the Peke's fund of energy is remarkable, his endurance likewise. I do not know why he is naturally more rugged, more vigorous than the average toy. Possibly it is because he does not wear himself out barking. I believe he is the quietest of all the small fry; undoubtedly that is one reason why hotel proprietors upon occasion have admitted him as a guest when they have refused so many others. He barks at the proper time and with reason, at other times outsiders would scarcely know he was around.

As a watchdog he scores because he barks when necessary to give the alarm. A senseless barker attracts little enough attention (save that of annoyance), because he is always at it, scraping his throat until he loses his voice and wears himself threadbare. An alert watchdog like the Peke, on the other hand, notifies all and sundry when something questionable is afoot, but only then.

So small a dog though, the objector might suggest, is not formidable enough to attack a burglar or protect a home. That is exactly where the objector would be wrong! The Peke has not the jaw strength comparable with that of many another dog, but do not forget that, being undershot, he has at his command the true lock-grip which he has been known to use quite effectively to fasten upon an intruder. The redoubtable Peke hurls himself bodily at a foe of whatever size and hangs on to the extreme discomfiture of his thieving host. This is neither theory nor breed propaganda, but cold, stark fact! It has happened and it will happen again just so long as there are Pekes trained to responsibility for home and property.

Brought to my attention is a case of a toy dog used as a guard which involved a Pekingese given the freedom of a farm where valuable tools and heavy implements lay about in a field right along a well travelled road. Electric light wires were being installed when at the end of the day, rather than re-load their equipment on the truck, the men pushed into the field a wire-drum mounted on its own wheel-body. The Peke in question never turned a hair as she sat and watched the men park the wire-drum in the field, but next morning she refused to let them take it out again! In disregard of her own safety, she charged at their legs until in exasperation the men tramped up to the house, fuming, "Lady, get that little vixen in so we can go on with our work!"

Such incidents are not unusual. Countless others can be related by Pekingese owners whose dogs have had an opportunity to absorb training and to develop initiative. In the perfect watchdog, size means little. It's the stout little heart of him that counts, and the courage, and the protective instinct which the Pekingese possesses to marked degree.

Small size, though, in itself can be an asset. It means, for one thing, comparatively less feeding expense; for another, the ability to smuggle the dog in oftentimes where the larger dog cannot go. A small dog is preferable for the little folks, too; he cannot knock them down in rough play. And if he has to be carried, or if someone wants to carry him around just for fun, he is only a comfortable armful.

Lapdog? I have already said *no* to that accusation, for the word, as used today, implies uselessness. The Peke is not by preference a lapsitter, yet there he will sit in courteous acquiescence if there seems enough reason for him to do so, as for instance when riding in the car or when enjoying himself on the porch. But how he likes the touch, the feel of master or mistress, hence of his own volition he sits close beside, every once in a while nudging with his body as if to say, "I'm right here if you need me."

His affection is limitless, but it is not inconsiderately offered. In fact, characteristically he is rather slow to respond, but when he does he is your unalterable friend for life.

Tri.-Int. Ch. Remenham Derrie represents the courage of the Lion Dog. He came by boat the long way to avoid submarines and was delayed by rough seas. The ship docked late Sunday; the show opened the next morning. We had no idea how he would act in the ring after such a trip and with strangers. Here was a test of character. Derrie stepped into the ring as if he owned it and won Best of Breed over the then top winning Peke.

S. Av Ouen Teu Tang. Illustrating past type. Shown with Frances Mary Weaver of Sutherland Av fame.

S. Av T-Ouen, past type.

Ch. Nia Jai Niki of Orchard Hill, illustrating the present.

4

Pekingese Past and Present

During the past few generations dog breeding has grown to surprising proportions. All sorts of people are engaged in it, some as a business for intrinsic return, others as a hobby which seems to interest as does nothing else. Whatever the motive, one thing is certain: dogs are being produced today in numbers greater than ever before, and in quality good, bad and indifferent.

Side by side with numerical increase in dogs and breeders has gone a like rapid increase in scientific knowledge of heredity, medicine and general handling. So it would seem as a natural consequence that dogs of all breeds should grow better, at least in show quality, as they grow greater in numbers. This is not the case.

In any breed, a quick rise to public favor is attended with great risk because so many, who are totally unqualified in knowledge and perseverance, join the ranks of the leading breed to get out of it what they can in cash or prestige. Hence, the moment a breed hits the peak of popular approval and becomes a fad, its general average of quality tends to deteriorate. Any matron is bred to any sire. As a result of ill conceived matings, strains are garbled beyond recognition, while valued characteristics, which sound breeders fought for and obtained only through years of patient effort, disappear in the melee of over-production.

Fortunately, the Pekingese has never been a fad. Slowly, but steadily, the dog rose to high place in the public esteem, and he has held that place year after year. At no time has he suffered eclipse in popularity and at no time has he been over-produced. This is about the happiest state of affairs a breed can enjoy. It means that its sponsors are breeding wisely, in considered moderation. It means that, the demand for the Pekingese is being maintained at a satisfactory level; that the improvement in quality is improvement of the *average,* which is the sole yardstick of breed progress.

About the only way a breed can be advanced steadily toward perfection is by establishing definite strains. What exactly is a strain? To put it simply, a strain is a line of descent; a collection of individuals incorporating certain distinguishing characteristics. By breeding within the family, in other words by line breeding, it is possible to establish a strain. Our earlier Pekingese fanciers established such strains and fixed by heredity the shorter nose and the overnose wrinkle of today. Few present-day breeders have the requisite patience for developing a strain of their own. They want quick results and either import a winner or buy from a fellow breeder. In America there are not many true strains for the original Pekingese kennels founded here around 1911 have dispersed and the influence of their dogs is so far back in some pedigrees as to be negligible.

From an old 1914 catalog, I note that Mrs. Harby exhibited fifteen Pekes, Mrs. Halley nine, and the list of exhibitors for that specialty show reads like the New York Social Register. Two famous names of an earlier date are Pierpont Morgan and his winning Ch. Cragston Sing, a grandson of Sutherland Avenue Ouen Teu Tang, and James Gordon Bennet, the club president, had five of his dogs illustrated in that catalog. "Sir" Charles Hopton was superintendent of the show which was held in the Ballroom of the Plaza Hotel in New York. Miss Lydia Hopkins judged an entry of 289, shown by seventy-one exhibitors. There are ninety-one pages in the profusely illustrated catalog which lists a club membership of 177. Breeders who followed these pioneers included Mrs. Harry Sears with her Wu Kees, the Greenwich Kennels of Mrs. F. Y. Mathis, the Herbert Mapes and their Whitworths, the McAllisters, also Mrs. Christian Hager and her famous Chu Chows. The strains they built in the East, did yeoman service for the breed.

As their well known lines faded from the scene, along came others. Let me mention a few of them. Mrs. Michael Van Beuren, Pekingese Club president for many years, owned the Sunnyfield Kennels at Newport, Rhode Island. Her winners came from leading English strains, plus one that I particularly remember as I bred him and showed him for her. He was her coal black Pier Wan Li of Orchard Hill. He finished for the title under that breeder-judge, Mrs. Harry Sears. Mrs. Sidney Franc had many Glen Iris homebred winners. Mr. & Mrs. Frank Downing had outstanding imports that, combined with America's bloodlines, produced many champions for their Hollylodge Kennels. Their Morris & Essex winner I especially admired, their homebred Ch. Wundah, whose brilliant career was cut short by a sudden tragic death. Mrs. Bertha Hanson is well remembered for her O'Palarts. Mrs. James Austin imported some of England's best stock and bred winners at Catawba for many years. Her most famous dog was Ch. Che Le of Matsons, known to us as "The Duck," a beautiful compact red and a great showman. He had to his credit many Best-in-Show wins. It was a real loss to the breed when he failed to sire. When Mrs. Austin died, her dogs died also. It was a breed tragedy when her veterinarian was ordered to put them to sleep.

After Catawba closed, Ruth Sayres, the kennel manager, showed Poodles for Mrs. Saunders Meade, and later through Ruth, Mrs. Meade became interested in Pekingese and bought the very beautiful English Ch. Caversham Ko Ko of Shanruss. I saw and applauded his sensational Best-in-Show win 1955 over 2294 dogs at Westchester. This glorious dog met an untimely end when he suffocated in the office during a kennel fire. A tragic loss to our breed. Fortunately, he was spared the agony of burning to death. Smoke inhalation put him to sleep.

Miss Sara Hodges was noted for her fine American-breds, and as to a *strain*, I believe she could claim that over a number of others since she did not import dogs. Her champions came from planned matings in her own family tree and were noted for beautiful heads and sturdy body conformation. She had a consistent winner in Ch. Yo Ling, the 1939 specialty best of breed. Later, her Ch. Tai Chuo's Son kept the colors flying by winning the specialty at Westchester. Due to ill health this kennel closed some years ago.

At the Misses Lowthers' Clamarlow Kennels, other specialty show

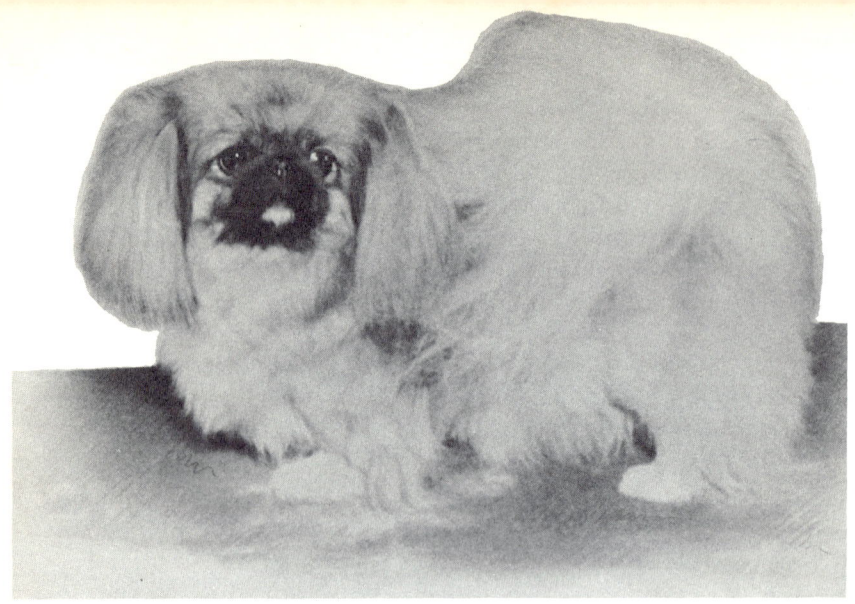

Ch. Kai Lo of Dah Lyn, 5 times Best in Show, 61 groups. Greatest winning bitch of her day, bred by John Royce.

Ch. Kai Jin of Caversham. Imported by John Royce. Best in Show 15 times and sired many champions.

winners were Ch. Silver Dust and his son Ch. Silver Star. There were six generations of homebreds back of them. Silver Dust won the summer specialty twice. His dam I am proud to say was a daughter of Ch. Jai Son Fu and was bred by Mrs. Evelyn Ortega. Charlotte Dempsey bought her from Mrs. Ortega and from a mating to the Lowthers' Coal Dust bred two champions, her own Ch. Star Dust II, and the Lowthers' Ch. Silver Dust. They were similar in type to Jai Son, with black masks, correct overnose wrinkles, great width of muzzles, level lips and wide flat top skulls. Any breeder coming to Orchard Hill can spot a Jai Son descendant by checking the head points mentioned. The Clamarlow Kennel closed after the death of Margaretta, Miss Clara's sister.

The Dah Lyn Kennels established in 1929 by John Royce and his sister, Caroline, have had prolonged success in the show ring. After his sister married "Jack" took over all the dogs and from his knowledge of pedigrees and planned breedings came many important winners for him and for others. His original stock combined Remenham, Nanking, Caversham, etc. In my opinion, his best homebred was a bitch, Ch. Kai Lo by Ch. Kai Lung of Remenham. She won everything in her day including Best in Show over Mr. Austin's famous Fox Terrier, Ch. Nornay Saddler. One can only regret she was not a male and thus more able to perpetuate her type. Never hesitating to breed outside his kennel, Jack used famous champions of complementary bloodlines and in one instance bred the youngest Pekingese champion to win Best in Show at our specialty, namely Ch. Jai Bee of Dah Lyn, whose dam was Remenham and sire was Ch. Jai Son Fu. His death while still a youngster was a real loss to the breed. Jack can rattle off more pedigrees per minute than all the rest of us put together. He knows *our* pedigrees as well as his own and this knowledge has made Dah Lyn one of our leading kennels. His Ch. Kai Jin of Caversham was Best in Show fifteen times and sired many champions. Mr. Royce continues to import and apparently gets a big kick out of showing a new one. He is famous for putting his dogs down in perfect condition and can groom to perfection. Lately, he has added more Alderbourne, Calartha, and Elsdon bloodlines and from them I am sure he will breed champions for years to come.

In New England, famous kennels of the past were owned by Mrs. Hadaway and Mrs. Julia French Williams who with their Heskeths

Mrs. Charmian Lansdown with Ch. Cha Ming Tang Wu of Kel Lee and sire Cha Ming Tang Wu.

Ch. Caversham Kai Ku of Pendarvis with owner, Mrs. Lola Brooks.

Ch. Chik T'sun of Tien Hia, by Ch. Chik T'sun of Caversham, bred by Mrs. Brooks.

and other champions kept interest alive and stimulated competition at their New England specialty club shows. Some of my first dogs were purchased from Mrs. Williams. Int. Ch. San Dee of Hesketh, Ch. Grey Spider of Hesketh and Ch. Cleo of Sunnyholme, bred by Mrs. Williams, were a few of the early dogs which subsequently became Orchard Hill champions. The New England specialty is no longer in existence, which is unfortunate since there are a great many new breeders in that section. How well I remember their colorful shows, with individual spaces roped off with ribbons gaily decorated with Chinese brocades and flowers, prizes offered for the best decorated baskets, etc. English clubs often put on shows of this type. Now the Blue Hills Pekingese Club of Massachusetts has in a way replaced the New England specialty. They hold their shows in conjunction with the Ladies Dog Club every June.

Mrs. Murray Brooks of Tien Hia fame, who has been breeding winners for a long time, has winning stock in every section of the country as well as her own champions in Texas. Her homebreds go back to early Pekingese history in America, to some of her original importations such as Ch. Sundah of Chinatown. Years ago, she bought an imported dog from me, Ch. Remenham Tombo of Orchard Hill, sire and grandsire of many champions not only in the Southwest, but at Orchard Hill and elsewhere. Among Mrs. Brooks' best known homebreds of the past was Ch. Tom Bo's Diamond which annexed his title in three shows and at one of them went on to win Best in Show all breeds! Diamond's son, Diamond Star, soon followed his illustrious sire and easily gained the title. This dog, "Star," Mrs. Brooks considered to be one of the best in quality she had bred up to that time. She should know as she is nationally recognized as an authority and is one of our best breeder-judges. Both dogs resulted from a well-planned outcross, as Ch. Remenham Tombo sired Diamond whose dam came from a long line of producing homebreds. Another successful stud at Tien Hia was Ch. Ku Che, by Ku Chuo of Orchard Hill. Mrs. Brooks was so anxious to secure Ch. Ku Chi of Caversham bloodlines that she stopped here on the way home from New York and took with her the line-bred four-weeks-old Ku Chuo whose sire and dam were by Ch. Ku Chi of Caversham. I had brought Ku Chuo's dam home with me in whelp when I judged the British Pekingese Championship show in the Spring of 1949. Incidentally, I awarded the challenge certificate and Best in Show to that same supreme little showman, Ch. Ku Chi of Caversham. Mrs. Brooks successfully hand-fed Ku Chuo on the long journey to Texas by using canned milk, a tablespoon and medicine dropper, and a cigarette lighter to heat the spoonful of milk. Her efforts were not in vain since he turned out to be a great stud dog. To further line-breed her Caversham stock, she imported Ch. Khi Ku of Pendarvis by Ch. Caversham Ku Ku of Yam. Khi Ku sired eleven champions including my Ch. Orchid Lanes Ku Lee. Unfortunately for the breed, Khi Ku died of a heart attack in 1963, but left many grandchildren that will win and add more luster to his name.

Mrs. Charmian Lansdowne, whose internationally known kennel is situated in California, has been breeding champions for more years than most of us. She brought her English dogs to this country around 1930. From them she bred numerous Cha Ming winners combining English bloodlines plus Wu Kee and other strains, and in later years, added Orchard Hill and Jaison bloodlines. She has consistently produced top dogs from this combination, not alone for herself, but for others as well, for she has sent Cha Ming champions into all parts of the West and South. Her dogs were well balanced, with profuse coats, grand heads, and always put down in perfect bloom and noted for their showmanship.

Mrs. Sears' Ch. Rajah of Hesketh was a consistent winner not only in the East, but Midwest and when we all met at the same Midwest shows it was more of a circus than a circuit—how we battled it out! In those days we really had fun, and competition it seems did not engender the bitter feelings and jealousies we sometimes encounter today. Lola Brooks, Stella Quick, Helen Shaftel, Ann Loring and Marie Plankers, all in one class, would make any judge wring his hands and cry for help!

Some later kennels in this locality include those of Mrs. Mary Hug of Chicago who has Orchard Hill and Yu Sen Yu Toi bloodlines in her pedigrees. I believe she was one of the few breeders in the Midwest to own a Tri-International champion. Her Jai Son Fu grandson, Ch. Cha Ming Mr. Kim of Ma Hu, made the title in this country, Canada and Mexico. He was bred by the late Mrs. Edna Fogel of California. Kim was named for his sire, a famous stud on the Coast, but he resembled his grandsire in head and type, and carried a magnificent coat. He sired outstanding show stock for Mrs. Hug and had winning progeny owned by other breeders.

Mrs. Peggy Bielot's Punchinello Kennels, well-known in Detroit since the late 1930s, had as one of her foundation bitches a daughter of my Ch. Kim's Tzu Shan. A good producer, she was dam of Ch. Gay Feathers which resembled Shan. Gay Feathers, a grand stud as well as showman, sired Punchinello Kim's Me—two champions I saw make some nice wins years ago in Detroit. Mrs. Bielot's homebred champions are a credit to a sincere breeder. She is still showing and breeding good ones.

Another kennel in Detroit with founding stock from here is owned by Adele and Marilyn Butkus. Mrs. Butkus has been raising Pekes for over twenty years and is helped now by her daughter Adele. Many of their dogs are down from Jai Son and Remenham Derrie. Their kennel name is Golden Gay.

Some early Midwestern owners such as Mrs. Muriel Freyman of Pekeholme fame preferred to breed show dogs and sell them, to let new owners have the worry or the fun as it may be of making them champions. Mrs. Freyman imported some of England's best and knows, as all the old timers do, that the strength of a kennel lies in its bitches. Her own champion bitches have contributed much to her success. She imported one bitch in whelp to Ch. Bonraye Fo Yu and had a litter of six by him before he came to me from England. Those she sold from that litter were great producers. From the Fo Yu son she kept came other winners and champions. By her tally and mine, I believe Fo Yu produced more winning children and grandchildren than any import to that date. There are quite a few breeders in this part of the West whose dogs I have not seen. I have no data on pedigrees or wins except as noted in the American Kennel *Gazette*. All I can say to them is "Congratulations!"

Mrs. Daniel Goodwin had some very good Pekes when I knew her years ago, and champions bred by her won in keenest competition. Her pedigrees were predominantly Orchard Hill. From a *Gazette* show report I note that her Ch. Goodwin's Tombo Cleo Dawn was sold to Mrs. R. W. Hamilton, who operates the well known Odell Pekingese Kennels in Kalamazoo. Mrs. Hamilton featured a champion some years ago whose picture was that very good Ch. Yu Sen Ra Le of Odell. From the name I assume he is a grandson of Ch. Bonraye Fo Yu. The Midwest's Mrs. Amber Darville, better known as Tri State Kennels, bred winners over a long period of time. She purchased her original stock from me. One of her best known studs was Pier Shimerh of Orchard Hill whose last recorded champion was Tri State Ching Boi. Pier Shimerh was by Pierson by Tri Int. Ch. Pierrot. For a son of his to win in 1954 shows what stamina and longevity some sturdy Pekingese do possess. Ch. Tri State Ching Boi won five points at Evergreen State Pekingese Club specialty and was bought by Mrs. Zara Smith of Seattle. I note the dam is Jai Son's Jaina so this dog must combine Jai Son and Pierrot bloodlines.

Others in the limelight in the Midwest were Mrs. N. E. Leedy of Argos, Ind. Her homebred stock included Ch. Jai Son Fu blood and combined with top English outcrosses such as her later star, Ch. Wei Puff of Pekeholme, she bred many winners. Wei Puff was from Mrs. Freyman's astute breeding a grandson of Ch. Bonraye Fo Yu. Mrs. J. Gimbel, also in Ohio, built up a small kennel to show status with such sires as Ch. Mi Ti Mite of Pekeholme, he too, was a Fo Yu grandson.

There are many small kennels of serious breeders unknown to me. But judging by AKC registrations in that area there must be innumerable show dogs produced whose owners are content to let them remain "back yard champions" rather than take on the expense and the risks of exhibiting. I offer my apologies for ignorance of their names, hence for not mentioning them. These should consider the Biblical saying, "Do not hide your light under a bushel."

Mrs. Herbert Mapes bred Pekingese for about twenty-five years. Her Witworth Kennels produced American-bred champions over a long period of time. Few imported dogs were needed to keep up quality in this establishment. However, many Whitworth homebreds were mated to imported studs so that the Whitworth line combined Pagan Chieftain blood and Arellian Choo Leen, while their last champion, Peer of Whitworth, goes back on the dam's side to Orchard Hill. Mrs. Mapes, who was one of our few good Pekingese artists, painted many famous representatives of the breed including those used in this book. She has captured in color the true likeness and correct modern type of most of our great champions, perpetuating them in lasting portraits for all posterity to see. When the Mapes disbanded their kennel and went to live in North Carolina, we missed them very much, and we kept hoping they would resume their former activities and return once again to our Pekingese circles.

Unfortunately, Mrs. Mapes passed away in the Spring of 1955. Herbert Mapes spent his last years with their niece, Mrs. Fortune Roberts of Bronxville, New York. Mrs. Roberts grew up with Pekingese and is one of our best known judges.

Mrs. Everett Clark, Poundridge, N.Y. has another well known strain of American-breds going back to Mrs. Sears' Hesketh dogs, and since then she has bred Miralac champions of finest quality. One of her first great winners, Ch. Major Mite of Miralac, was a well balanced small dog with the profuse coat characteristic of the Heskeths. His son, Ch. Ho Yan of Miralac was sold to Mrs. Nathan Wise of Cincinnati. This dog became a champion in his own right and a producer as well, for he sired Ch. Major Mite of Honan which did such phenomenal winning for Mrs. Wise. He corralled not alone some best toy wins, but won Best in Show at our Pekingese Club specialty of 1949, and previous to that won an all-breed Best in Show in the Middle West. His profuse coat goes back to the Hesketh dogs from Mrs. Clark. Mated to other good bitches belonging to Mrs. Wise, Major Mite blood soon established for her a strain of homebreds destined to produced more champions and added luster for Bond Hill. This kennel closed after Pauline Wise died, but other Midwest breeders are still winning with her stock.

Mrs. Evelyn Ortega established her Rosedown Kennels about the time Ch. Jai Son Fu was making a name for himself. Some of her finest and best producing stock came from that breeding and gave her a Jai Son daughter which was the dam of two champions. She also bred to Tri. Int. Ch. Remenham Derrie and had winning stock from him. His daughter, Plum Blossom, is the dam of her Ch. Derrie of Rosedown. I cannot list all her homebred champions, but I know they came from a combination of bloodlines, her own and Orchard Hill, Whitworth and Dah Lyn. Of late years quite a few imports have been winning for her. Rosedown is now located in Connecticut, where she has a most attractive place in the country near Norwalk.

Other kennels of this period include the well-known Del Vilas, owned by two sisters, Mrs. Justin Herold and Miss Delphine McEntyre. They have been breeding and showing for many years and have been very successful with their homebreds. Bloodlines there go back to Cha Ming and Hesketh, including the lovely small Ch. Wee Jock of Hesketh and others so prominent in show pedi-

Ch. Orchid Lanes Ku Lee, winning under Mr. Royce. Ku Lee won Best in Show Specialty 1960–1962.

Ch. Bu Ku of Kaytocli, owned by Mrs. Everett Clark.

Ch. Zarietta, imported, and Ch. U Toy Mei, a Derrie granddaughter, bred by Mrs. Ortega.

Jai Minx and Jai Chu Pao, by Ch. Jai Son, bred and owned by Mrs. Ortega.

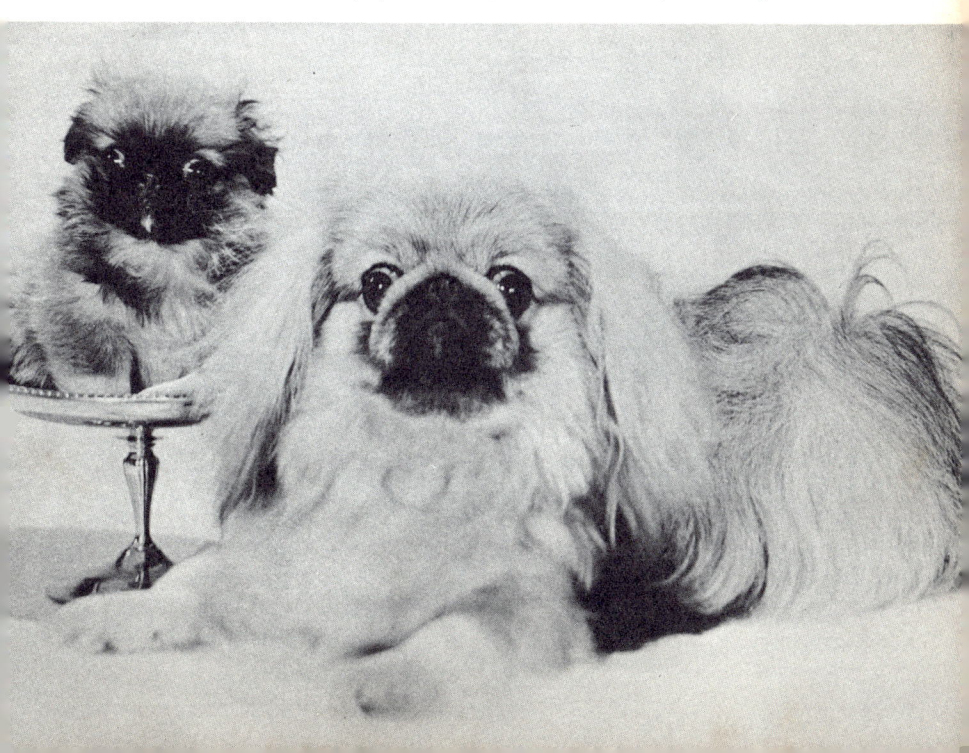

grees of those days. In 1952, they had winners bitch at the New York specialty show with a Ch. Son Fu daughter. They also had winning daughters by Ch. Fei-Jai-Son, in fact, the 1953 futurity puppy dog and bitch were sired by him. The Del Vila dogs were not shown often, but now back in the ring they are winning with homebreds from imported bloodlines, Caversham, etc., and finished several lovely champions in 1963. Their recent stars are Ch. Del Villa Debonaire and Glamour Girl and their beautiful Ch. Del Vila Ku Chi Tu. Both sisters take an active part in show and club affairs not alone in Pekingese, but in other events in their section. I believe Miss McEntyre is president of the Saw Mill Kennel Club of White Plains. Both are popular and well known judges not only of toy dogs, but of many other breeds.

Another small kennel in New York is Millrose, owned by Mrs. Edwin Blamey, wife of one of our best known veterinarians. Dr. Blamey has been associated with the Pekingese Club of America as far back as I can remember. I note he was official veterinarian in the 1920 show catalog. He is president of the Pekingese Club of America and our delegate to the AKC. The Blameys have a place on Long Island where Mrs. Blamey has a few choice dogs with "Quality" her motto. She is best known today as the breeder-owner of Ch. Millrose Ballerina the outstanding bitch winner of our 1951 Westchester summer specialty, and best toy there. She reminds me of her grandsire—the same head points as Ch. Jai Son Fu. Her sire, Mrs. Dempsey's Ch. Star Dust II, is out of a Jai Son daughter. Mrs. Blamey also bred Ch. Millrose Hornet and many other winners.

Mrs. Dorothy Dwyer Hanson, also of Long Island, was an active breeder some years ago. We all remember her wins with "Chubby" and the good particolors she bred. I understand she keeps only a few dogs now, but is doing her share of winning and successfully campaigned Ku's Kin of West Winds to his title.

Mrs. de la Torre Bueno and her daughter, Iris, our very capable club secretary, raised Pekingese many years ago, but gave them up; their All-Celia kennel is famous today for their champion Brussels Griffons. Mrs. Horace Wilson of Wilton, Connecticut has West Winds, one of our newer kennels which although not large is all quality. She has bred many champions, and supports the shows in the New York area. She has done lots of winning with her Ch. Alderbourne Tong Tello, and with progeny from her Ch. Tong Tuo of

Ch. Del Vila Debonaire, by Ch. Calartha Yen Lo of Sua Lane out of Del Vila Flower Drum Song.

Ch. Del Vila Glamor Girl, by Ch. St. Aubrey Jin T'sun of Holmvallee out of Del Vila Glamor Girl.

Ch. Ko Ko of Westwinds, by Ch. Tong Tuo of Pekeboro, breeder-owner Mrs. Horace Wilson.

Pekeboro. Mrs. Wilson is also a well known and popular judge here and abroad. Mrs. Marion Vega of N. Y. City has a small kennel of show dogs and supports our specialty shows. She is breeding some nice whites at this time.

Pekestone, owned by Mrs. Dan Mosher of Buffalo, was a small kennel of really top show dogs, unknown perhaps to some breeders, but with stock from Orchard Hill plus an imported Moonland female, Pekestone made an enviable record. Mrs. Mosher purchased Shang, a son of our Ch. Kims Tzu Shan and made him a champion. From him, out of Minty of Moonland, came Pepper of Pekestone, one of the greatest sires of his time. This dog of massive head and grand type would have been an easy champion, but before he could complete his title, distemper wrecked an eye and finished his show career. Pepper sired our Ch. Jai Nee out of a Ch. Jai Son Fu daughter; he sired as well Ch. Shanga Salle and Ch. Gem of Pekestone, all three bitches being Pekingese Club champions as well as AKC champions. He sired other champions not owned here, and is grandsire of Ch. Piazza's Peppermint, which won Best in Show years ago on the Coast.

Mrs. Mosher also bred another great stud of championship caliber, although unknown to some. His name was Tombo's Tim of Pekestone, by Tombo of Orchard Hill by Ch. Remenham Tombo. Tim, as he was called, sired Ch. Narda of Orchard Hill, and Ch. Posy of Pekestone, later owned by Mrs. Brooks. He also sired Ch. Minty of Orchard Hill, and Minty of Pekestone which could have won her title if shown. Credit should be accorded Mrs. Mosher and her producing studs which did so well in so short a time. The death of Mr. Mosher meant the closing of the Pekestone Kennels. Orchard Hill purchased all the Pekestone dogs and continued to breed them along the same lines.

Several kennels that have had stock from here belong to Mrs. Harold Spicer, who shows occasionally in the Rochester area. Myrtle Raczinski not only shows in Upper New York, but has done very well at our Pekingese Club specialties and now with Mrs. Wilson's bloodlines has several Westwind champions. Mrs. Arthur Gowie of Troy is a new breeder and in stiff competition showed to the title her lovely Ch. St. Aubrey Marianne of Elsdon, bred by Bertha Smith.

In New York State there are quite a few small kennels whose owners keep only a dozen or so Pekes and show occasionally as is the case in all sections of the country. I cannot write about them all as much as I would like to. I sincerely hope these smaller kennels continue to breed good dogs and support as many shows as they can. In doing so they are keeping our breed before the public eye and insuring its continued popularity.

A larger kennel that did remarkably well in a short time was that of Mrs. Herbert Katz of Syracuse and her Roh Kai dogs. Her well-built kennels were opened in 1952, and she was exhibiting at our New York specialty the following year. She began with a few house pets and, living in the midst of a show-giving club area, she became interested in breeding better dogs and in showing them. In 1950, she came to Orchard Hill where she purchased a pair of show puppies. The male gained his title without difficulty in 1952. He is Ch. T'Jai Mi of Orchard Hill, a Jai Son grandson and a good stud. He sired Ch. Roh Kai Jai Mi's Shad and Ch. Roh Kai Iwon Jing, which were two of Mrs. Katz's best young homebreds. In the purchase of Mao Ling of Dah Wong, Mrs. Katz had the rare good luck of an outcrossed breeding and, using Mrs. Voyle's Ch. Wardene Sun Fo, she raised three of that litter to championship status. The mating of Mao Ling, which also became a champion, to Ch. T'Jai Mi also produced two champions. Certainly an auspicious beginning which again points up the fact that producing bitches are of utmost importance to a kennel. Good bitches *make* a kennel, with few studs really needed if one is willing to go outside and pay the fee for a male known as a producer.

Mrs. Katz handled her own dogs and made many of them champions. Her first entries at our Pekingese Club of America show were in January, 1953; then in 1954 she won best male puppy with T'Jai Mi Shad, and futurity bitch puppy with his sister, Roh Kai Iwon Jing. She had nice wins with her first homebreds, then augmented her stock by importing through Nigel Aubrey Jones her well known English winner of 1953, Ch. Aubrey Kimona of Tzumio. He quickly made his title and enjoyed a great victory of Best in Show at Dunkirk, New York. This win was repeated in 1955 by her imported Wei Tiko of Pekeboro. Before export to this country, Tiko had gained the Junior Warrant as had my own Ch. Kai Lung of Vinedeans, and in America both dogs made their championships in short order. Mrs. Katz' wins of best of breed at Westminster and Best in Show at Dunkirk were of course a great thrill for her; they

Ch. St. Aubrey Marianne of Elsdon, owned by Mrs. Arthur Gowrie.

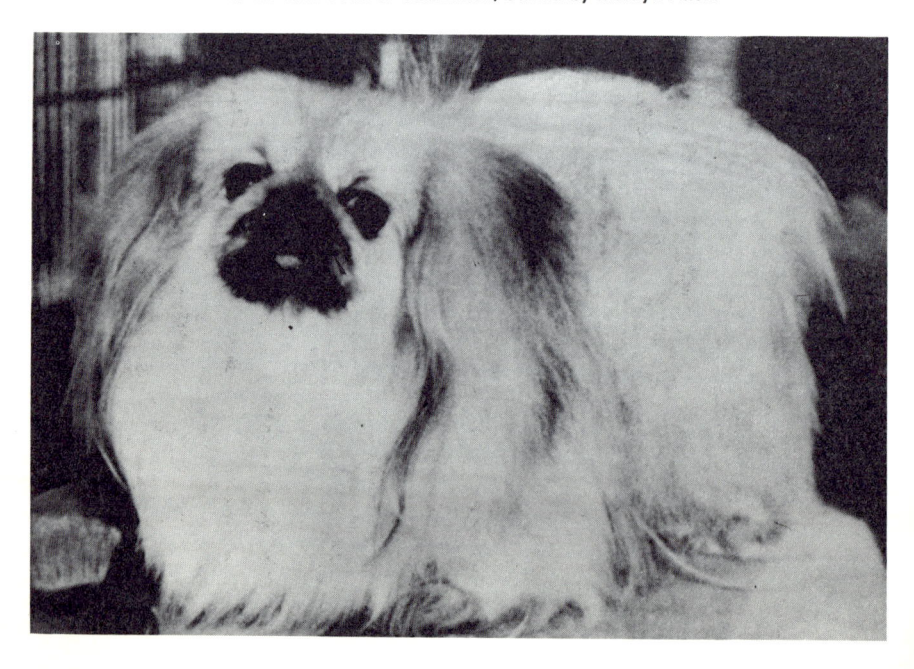

Int. Ch. Chik T'sun of Coronation, owned by Marilyn Allen.

should be as well an incentive to new breeders since they prove what perseverance and sincere interest in the breed can accomplish. Within ten years she had campaigned fourteen Pekes to their titles, and since then others of her bloodlines have become champions. Mrs. Katz was greatly assisted by her husband, Dr. Herbert Katz, an eye specialist. All who breed Pekingese know the need for constant attention to the eyes, as eye trouble is a breed weakness. The Roh Kai dogs were all sold by Dr. Katz after Rose Marie suffered a paralyzing stroke in 1960.

An older and serious breeder in New England is Mrs. Marilyn Allen whose Coronation Kennel is well known to all of us. One of her beautiful homebreds is Ch. Coronation Jai Jin. She also bred Int. Ch. Chik T'Sun of Coronation and his son, Ch. Jin Jin. Her dogs are noted for their lovely coats and correct type. They are put down in perfect condition. Her kennel ads read and justly so, "The Coat Kennel of the East."

Newer kennels in New England belong to Mrs. Ester Martin who is breeding show dogs from Dah Lyn and imported bloodlines.

Mrs. Edith Smith's Imperial Kennel owns Ch. Roh Kai Ti Chi, bred by Mrs. Katz. His Roh Kai breeding, combined with her homebreds is producing winners for her. Mrs. Alex Frank showed a very good black at the 1963 specialty and with stock from Westwinds will soon be in the winners circle. Jane Chester seems to be concentrating on good blacks and with stock from Ir Ma Mi should do very well. Emily Hennessey is building up a nice kennel of show dogs, mostly based on Coronation lines. The Haven Peke Inn Kennel owned by Marion Haven is a promising new one, plus many others which are listed in the Directory. Helen and Leo Hyder active in the Blue Hills Pekingese Club have raised very good dogs and we must not forget Geraldine Pearce and her Cavernocks. She raised many champions some years ago, but is not, we are sorry to say, an active breeder any more.

Kennels in New York include the up and coming Palace Guards, owned by William Blair and Lew Prince. They have stock from Mrs. Nell Bailey, combining Jehol, Caversham St. Aubrey and have several champions to their credit. They also have Ku Chi Cinda from Orchard Hill, needing one show to finish, and a very lovely young homebred, Palace Guard Pat-ti, surely another champion for them in 1964.

Mr. & Mrs. Roderick Nourse have been active breeders for many years and although they do not keep many dogs those they have are either champions or future ones. Their Twinkle of Dah Lyn was the top producing matron of 1963 with three champions to her credit. They were bred and shown to their titles from the bred-by-exhibitor class by Mrs. Nourse. Other dedicated breeders of this area are Mrs. Frank Hess, who raises show dogs in the home rather than in a regular kennel. Many of her winners are of "West Winds" bloodlines. Mrs. Eric Lagercrantz has imports that are champions as well as homebreds. Mary loves little ones and gets a great "kick" out of showing "Papoose" and Kai Lungs Be Be, a miniature daughter of Ch. Kai Lungs she bought from me.

Mrs. Marie Koch Zerman of Lebanon, Pennsylvania, bred Pekes for many years and with Orchard Hill stock bred two champions later owned by Mrs. Richard Bell. They were Ch. Bon Yu Fei Shawnee of Cal-Marie and Int. Ch. Jai Pier De Be, his son.

Mr. & Mrs. Richard Bell have a small but carefully built kennel of quality dogs in the rural section of Oradell, New Jersey. They started out with a few pets, but became interested in breeding show dogs so selected Orchard Hill stock as foundation. They bought Mi Chala of Orchard Hill and bred her to Ch. Feisal, and from this mating got their good red champion, Fei Mi Yenlo of Orchard Hill. Their dam, Mi Chala, won her title in hot competition; she was also a group winner as was her son, Yen Lo, which won a strong group at Philadelphia. They also did a lot of winning with Ch. Cho Sans Galant Man, bred as the name indicates, by Edna Voyles. Later, Mike Smith handled their dogs and through him they bought their present-day winner, Ch. Ming Lou Man Chu.

Mrs. Clifford Bailie of Hillcrest, Doylestown, Pennsylvania, had a beautiful male to head her kennel, Ch. Montgomery of Alderbourne, from the famous Ashton Cross line, and from him, with her good imported bitches purchased to breed to him, she has good show stock coming on. Mrs. Bailie recently imported Ku Ku of Fyldecoast by Ch. Man Stone Ku Yu of Mafasaga. He was best puppy at Crufts; now over here he is well on the way to his American title.

Another Pennsylvania kennel is the small one owned by Mrs. Laura Mosheim of Pottstown who began with Bonraye Fo Yu and Ch. Kai Lung stock, and is still breeding some very nice dogs. Her lovely Ch. Ku Bee is Alderbourne and Caversham and is the dam of

Ch. Mi Chala winning a group. Shown with Richard Bell and Mr. Royce who handled her for the Bells.

Ch. Ying T'sai, Ch. Dushka, Ch. Tobermory, Twinkle of Dah Lyn. Bred, shown to titles by owner, Agnes Nourse.

my Ch. Tul Ku Zac and granddam of other champions here. Mrs. Florence Gwynn of New Jersey has a small kennel of show dogs and champions. Some of them bred from Roh Kai stock. Her latest champion is Gwynnes Gai Ling which was greatly admired when she took winners bitch at our PCA specialty of 1963. We welcome a new exhibitor of Pekingese, Mrs. Walter Imrie. She is better known in Poodle circles, but had Pekes years ago as house pets and now is grooming, we hear, some exciting new show prospects.

Mrs. Elizabeth Delk of Point Pleasant, Pennsylvania, has been breeding good Pekingese for many years, but seldom shows now. She is also well known as a judge of toy dogs. Mr. and Mrs. Robert Zettle have a small kennel of show dogs nicely located on the outskirts of State College, Pennsylvania. Their kennel name is Springview and Mrs. Zettle is the breeder of Ch. Ku Lee's Tulya of Orchard Hill owned by Vernon Lorenzen of St. Paul. Tulya's granddam, Tul Ku Dena of Orchard Hill, needs one major for the title, but was bred and is shown here with her champion daughter and we hope champion granddaughter. As their names indicate, they are Ch. Tul Ku Zac breeding; Zac is by Tulyar of Alderbourne with Orchard Hill homebreds on their dam's side. Future top winners are bound to come from such a background.

The Raymond Smiths of Erie had the rare good fortune of getting Kai Lung Marie as foundation for their Ra Ene kennel. Marie is by Ch. Kai Lung of Vinedeans and Orchard Hill out of a line-bred Jai Son Fu bitch. They finished her in stiff competition and then brought her back to be bred to Ch. Nia Sing Tsu Jolity. The Smiths made two champions from Marie's first litter namely, Ch. Kai-Ty-Ko and Ch. Kai Kim and what is really remarkable, they finished at the same show. Quite an achievement! Later, they bought Jolity, a Sailor son, now needing a major to finish. His daughter, Nia Jo Holly of Ra Ene also has points and should have no trouble gaining brought back to be bred to Ch. Nia Sing Tsu Jolity. The Smiths also have a very good young show male in Dan Dee of Dahlyn as an outcross.

The William Gordons established their Pickering Forge Kennels near Philadelphia, with line-bred females from us and although a new kennel, they have done some nice winning and will surely have more champions this year. Their 1963 star, was Ch. Beaupres Kan Jin of Jamestown, a Ch. Ku Jin of Caversham grandson. They can

Ch. Shan Jin of Caversham, owned by Harold Frazer and A. Williams.

Ch. Beaupres Kan Jin of Jamestown, owned by Mr. & Mrs. Wm. Gordon.

Tul Ku Dena Fu Fu and Ch. Tul Ku Toya of Springview, owned by Mrs. Robt. Zettle.

Ch. Majara Mariner, bred and owned by Mrs. Dixon Lathrop.

now line breed Caversham stock, as they have Ch. Ku Lee bloodlines from here. The Gordons are very generous and have helped other breeders in times of distress including myself. They, with the help of their veterinarian, saved the life of an important matron of mine. They also support with good entries, the shows in this section as well as our specialty shows.

Another new kennel with startling success is "Majara," owned by Mrs. Dixon Lathrop. She is well known for her many famous Afghan champions, but fell in love with Pekingese "character" and in her first litter bred Ch. Majara Mariner. His sire was Ch. Nia Sing Tsu Jolity of Lyall, better known as Sailor. Mariner was aptly named for his sire as he, as well as his son, had a "Sailor's" correct rolling gait. His dam is Ch. Kim Toi's Lea of Orchard Hill, Mrs. Lathrop's second champion within a year.

Mrs. Hermine Cleaver of Delaware has a small kennel that combines Jai Son bloodlines plus Caversham and Alderbourne through my Ch. Ku Chi and Mrs. Mosheim's Ch. Ku Bee of Kents Hill. She had the thrill of winners bitch at our 1961 New York specialty with her Jai Atom Mieke of Orchard Hill, later a champion. She supports shows in her area as well as both specialties, and again had the thrill of winners dog at our 1964 winter Pekingese Club of America specialty show with her homebred Pencader Ku Kai Tim Meh. He is by Bettinas Kow Tow and is a grandson of our Ch. Kai Lung.

Down Baltimore way, we find Mrs. Gaston Remy, who supported our breed in that section and made competition keen indeed for northern dogs which ventured that far. Her kennel goes back to the 1930s. She bought a son of my Ch. Kims 'Tzu Shan when he was winning and made her "Shan" son a champion. His name was Ch. Shan Tung of Orchard Hill. From him, she bred winners including that grand bitch we all admired, namely Ch. Burma Lita. In turn, Lita produced several champions. Bred to Ch. Bonraye Fo Yu, Mrs. Remy got her Ch. Burma Toni, a grand-headed, typical dog that had scant difficulty gaining his title. He consistently won groups for her. Bred to Royce's Ch. Kai Jin of Caversham, Lita produced another lovely champion. Bitches like this are the backbone of any kennel and ordinarily not for sale at any price. Due to family illness, Mrs. Remy sold most of her dogs only retaining a few favorites as house pets.

New breeders in Maryland are many; most of them are listed in the Directory, but one that I think is particularly interesting is Och-K-Ma owned by Otto Harrup and Kerry Allen because they own not only AKC champions of record, but have obedience winners. They were the first to get a degree for their local club with their "Sheba"—Princess Diamond Rose CD went into their records with the first obedience title medal. Sheba is also a matron and had two litters of show prospects. Their Ch. Mickie Ash is an obedience winner and Prince with majors on his title is working on CDX (Companion Dog Excellent) and has twice received trophies for the highest scoring toy in the Richmond Club. Pekingese are notoriously stubborn and when they win top honors in obedience trials it is a real achievement and indicates the many hours of hard work put into it by the owners.

The Dragon Hai Kennels established a few years ago by Harold Frazer and Allen Williams have done very well in a short time. Their foundation bloodlines are primarily Caversham. Shan Jin of Caversham bred by Mary de Pledge made his title in keen competition. They say of him, "Shan is the only Caversham-bred dog in America out of two champion parents—Ku Jin of Caversham and Ch. Caversham Chik Ita of Swanbury." Their Shantung Fan by Ch. Shan Jin was winners bitch and best of winners, P. C. A. specialty March, 1964.

Bettina Belmont Ward is nationally known for her famous champions including "Kow Kow." She imported his beautiful mother, Black Queen of Orchard House, bred to Ch. Caversham Ku Ku of Yam. So, Kow Kow, although born here, is not classified as American-bred. He made his debut under me, his first group win then on to a spectacular show career, including best of breed at our summer specialty, Best in Show at the Progressive All Toy show not once, but thrice and where his dam Black Queen was best of opposite sex, a worthy champion in her own right. Kow Kow is shown here winning our specialty at Westchester. His record includes twenty-three times Best in Show and seventy-one group firsts. Mrs. Ward also did a lot of winning with Ch. Bay Li's Purple Passion (what a name) and Ch. Bay Li Shaman and recently imported a very good black and tan from Hindley Taylor, of Kyratown fame named Belgran Woo. How refreshing it is these days when colors other than fawns and reds get the winner's ribbon. Bettina's first

Ch. Bettinas Kow Kow, owned by Bettina Belmont Ward.

Ch. Mae's Woo Pe Kwo Choo, bred and owned by Mr. & Mrs. Charles Jordon; won Best of Opposite Sex, PCA Specialty, March 1964.

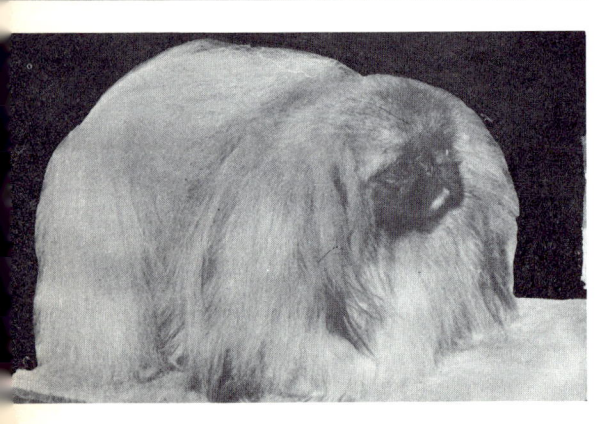

Bey Li Ku Jac, bred and owned by Mrs. Nell Bailey, sired by Ch. Chik T'sun of Caversham.

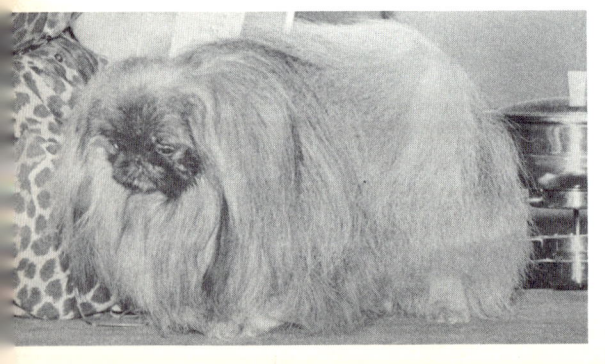

Ch. Mandarin's Kentucky Colonel, owned by Mrs. Ralph O'Daniel, bred by Penny Macklin.

champion bitch and still her house dog and favorite is the miniature she selected here, Ch. Kai Lungs Gem of Orchard Hill.

Mrs. Charles Jordan of Charlotte has had great success the last few years: eight champions to her credit including the beautiful brother and sister team, Ch. Mae's Woo Pe' Kwo Choo, the best of opposite sex winner at our Summer specialty, 1963, at Westchester. Ch. Maes Silver Sheenah, his sister, finished with three majors. Kwo Choo won best of breed at the Georgia specialty. They are by Ch. Chik T'sun out of Ch. Bettina's Cow Slip.

The Bey Li Pekingese of White Plains, Kentucky are noted for grand heads and profuse coats. Mrs. Bailey said, "I have bred show dogs for thirty years, have no idea how many champions came from my kennel. It has not been convenient to handle my own dogs, so I usually sell my "prospects" at an early age, which has done more for my name than if I had shown them myself. My best producing bitch, Bama Belle, is either wife, mother or grandmother of most of my dogs. She is a small bitch, sturdy as a pony and whelps almost as freely as she eats. She is a granddaughter of your Ch. Bonraye Fo Yu." Mrs. Bailey has sold most of her dogs to the A. P. Tarpley Kennel in Hermando, Mississippi. She is keeping only a few bitches and is retaining a small male by Ch. Chik T'sun of Caversham for stud service.

Mrs. Ralph O'Daniel, of Owensboro has carved a niche for herself in our Pekingese Hall of Fame, with that sensational winner, her Ch. Kentucky Colonel. Don't you love that name? I think it would be quite fitting if a good son of his is named Kentucky Bourbon! In one year of showing he won thirty group firsts, nine Best in Show awards and was the top winning Pekingese in the States for 1963. He is expertly handled by Lorraine Heichel of Cedar Lake, Indiana.

Houston and Peggy Carr have a well known kennel in Nashville, of Alderbourne background, known for good square heads and correct overnose wrinkles. Their Ch. Carrs Fabulous One is an outstanding example of our breed and is siring show stock.

Now we come to those well known winning "Cho Sens" owned by Mr. and Mrs. G. W. Voyles of Louisville. Their foundation stock goes back to Orchard Hill through Int. Ch. Sandman of Honan and Ch. Cho Cee of Marglo. These bloodlines combined with Ch. Wardene Sun Fo, their English stud, did exceptionally well for the

Voyles, meaning a combination of Yu Sen, Caversham, Alderbourne, then Calartha. I have no data on the number of champions bred, but I do know Edna finished a great many, not only Cho Sens, but champions for others. Top winners there today are Ch. Cho Sen Brite Mischief and his sire, Ch. Cho Sen Brite Future. Bright Mischief is Cho Sen's fourth generation of Best-in-Show winners as he achieved that feat in 1964. Edna is an artist, noted not only for her Pekingese paintings, but for the figurines she makes that are so lifelike they are startling. Hair is saved from the grooming brush and applied to a miniature clay model, complete in every detail. Even a live Peke will sniff at it to see if it's real!

Mr. and Mrs. J. B. Harp of Atlanta have raised Pekingese for many years. Their bloodlines were predominantly American. Two of their best known studs were Ch. Fu Shen of Dah Wong and Ch. Cho San Sing Lee. Mrs. Harp's handicap so bravely surmounted is perhaps not known to many. With her permission I mention it purely as tribute to her courage. She lost her right leg above the knee as well as a portion of her left foot. Her first Pekingese she named, "Dawn," because it was chosen to help shorten the long years ahead in a wheel chair. Shortly thereafter, she became deeply interested in the breed. Meantime, she learned to walk and associated with J. E. Hanger, Inc. went to business every day helping other amputees to get adjusted, and subsequently became one of the four women certified fitters of artificial limbs in this country. She also qualified as an AKC judge and did our summer specialty for us in 1956.

Another well known kennel of champions is owned by Mrs. Russell Inge, whose early dogs included Ch. Bond Hill Jay Ginger, also the English Canadian American Ch. St. Aubrey Judy of Calartha which they purchased from me. Incidentally, she was the only Pekingese bitch to stand as an English five CC (Challenge Certificate) winner and champion of three countries. Mrs. Inge has champions at stud with England's most famous bloodlines predominating. She also handles Pekingese and has won many titles.

Moving farther South, we find the large groups of English imports in the Midway Kennels owned by Mrs. F. J. Stubbart of Atlanta. She selected most of them personally in England not only for their show wins, but for their siring ability. Her Alderbourne bloodlines produced many winners for her and for others. We all wish Mrs. Stubbart would bring some of her lovely dogs North since so few of us have seen them. Another well known Southern kennel is owned by the Easton Hallmarks whose imports such as Ch. Chik Tu of Peperstiche have done their share of winning and siring champions. Chik Tu was imported by Mrs. Voyles then jointly owned by Mr. Hallmark and shown to the Tri-International title by Mrs. Voyles. A Hallmark winner is Ch. Misty Point Red Radiance.

The first show dogs owned by Mr. and Mrs. Charles Venable of Atlanta were Fo Yu of Orchard Hill, by Ch. Bonraye Fo Yu, then a winning daughter of Ch. Kai Lung of Vinedeans plus other American bloodlines. When they heard about Chik T'sun of Caversham being for sale, they bought him from Nigel Aubrey-Jones and then began his sensational show career, and sensational it really was. Clara Alford, the well known handler of toys, showed him from coast to coast and piled up a record never equalled by any other dog in our AKC history: 121 times Best in Show, 169 group firsts in the States, twenty-six group firsts in Canada, also eleven times Best in Show in Canada. "Chik" also holds the record for consecutive Best in Show wins, fourteen in a row within forty-six days. Then ran up eleven more consecutive Best in Show wins and climaxed all this by winning Best in Show at Westminster, February, 1960. Had he not been retired that night he could have broken his own 14th consecutive Best-in-Show wins. He was retired while still in his prime to become a great stud force and has sired many champions, which will leave a lasting impression on the breed. Chik T'sun is the only Pekingese ever to win the Garden.

A runner-up so to speak, happened in 1918, when "Sir Charles Hopton and Vinton Breese, the two judges approved to do Best in Show, could not agree. The Pekingese Ch. Phantom of Ashcroft, owned by Elbridge Gerry Snow, was favored by Mr. Hopton, but Mr. Breese preferred the *Bull Terrier,* Ch. Haymarket Faultless. They were deadlocked, so the show committee called in a referee, George Thomas, another judge, to make the final decision between the two dogs. Mr. Thomas awarded the Best in Show prize to the Bull Terrier. Old timers will always remember the "Elegant Sir Charles," so English, dressed to perfection and those fancy waistcoats! He and Vint Breese were quite a team and worked hard to make our breed popular in those early days. "The Pekingese Standard Simplified" was written and illustrated by Vinton Breese in

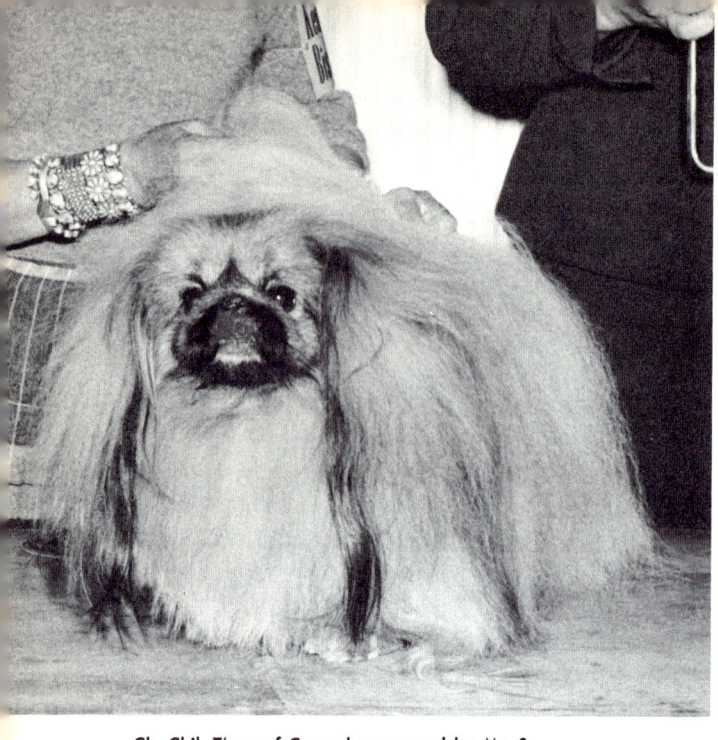

Ch. Chik T'sun of Caversham owned by Mr. & Mrs. Charles Venable, shown by Clara Alford.

Chik T'sun, with his owners.

1924. There is a picture of Ch. Phantom in it, the dog which almost won the Garden. Mr. Hopton gave me all his old catalogues of 1911. He told me he had owned at one time the painting by Maude Earl of Queen Victoria's Pekingese. Does anyone know where it is today?

Chik T'sun has passed on his quality, his good head points, and wonderful coat to his progeny. Two of the first well known kennels to breed to him were Mrs. Lola Brooks with the resulting Ch. Chik T'sun of Tien Hia, then Mrs. Marylin Allen and her lovely Ch. Chik T'sun of Coronation.

A comparatively new kennel in Georgia is Mrs. C. W. Austin's "Charoca." Here we find her beautiful Ch. Orchid Lanes Ku Lee T'sun. When Jack Watts gave up his dogs Mrs. Austin was lucky indeed to pick this Ku Lee son from a litter only two months old. I wish I had been with her as surely there must have been others in that litter of champion quality. I bred the dam of Ch. Ku Lee T'sun; Oberon's Judy by my Oberon of Elfann by Puff Ball of Chung king which sired Ch. Ku Chi of Caversham. So it was perfect line breeding as Ch. Orchid Lanes Ku Lee is by Ch. Khi Ku of Pendarvis by Ch. Caversham Ku Ku of Yam by Ch. Ku Chi of Caversham. I must have been away at the time Judy was sold or I would have bought her back. She is the nearest thing left that I know of to Puff Ball as Oberon her sire is gone. When I was in England, I bought my Elfann dogs from Miss Evans, an unassuming lovely person who will always be remembered in Pekingese history as the breeder of Miss de Pledge's Ch. Ku Chi of Caversham out of Marigold of Elfann.

Dixieland Plantation owned by Mrs. Gerald Livingston, of New York and Quitman, Georgia is a fabulous place not only for Pekingese and Poodles, but for Field Trial champions. The kennel name is "Kilsyth." They also raise prize cattle and walking Tennessee horses. Mrs. Livingston sends her friends a most intriguing desk calendar every Christmas depicting her winning dogs, horses, and house pets. She has done a lot of group winning with Int. Ch. Calartha Yen Lo of Sualane.

Mrs. P. M. McGoldrick, of Terra Ceia has an interesting kennel. She sent me this data: "I own Chik T'sun's Lone Ranger given to me by Mrs. Henry Brooks of Wah Bagin fame when she lived in Florida. Later, Mrs. Brooks bought his litter brother Chik T'sun Apache and had Clara Alford finish him. When Mrs. Brooks died

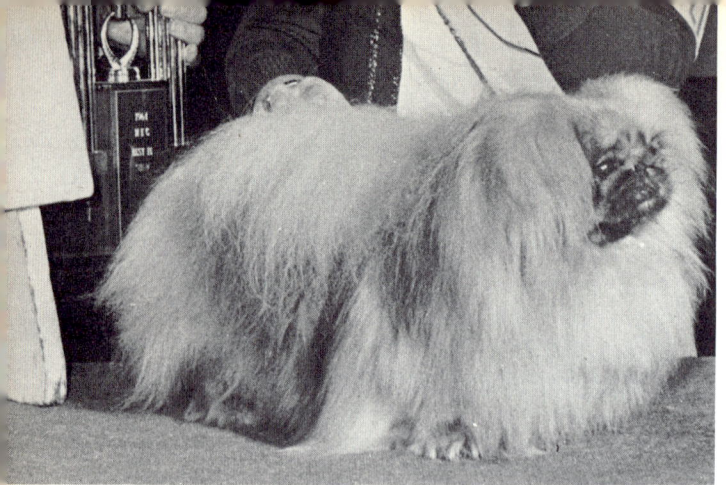

Ch. Cho Sen Brite Mischief, bred and owned by Mrs. G. W. Voyles. Her fourth generation of home bred Best in Show winners.

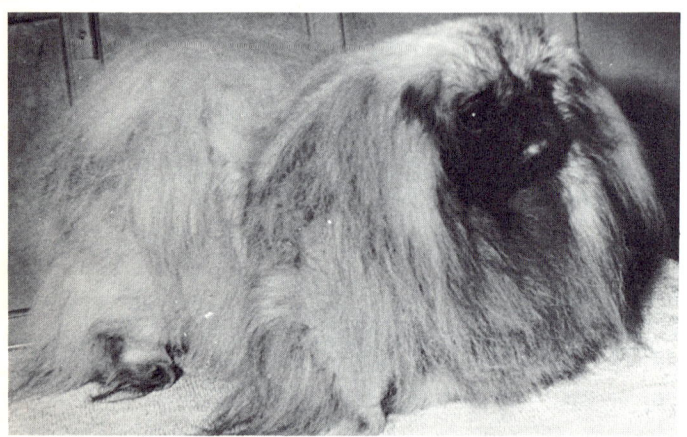

Ch. Orchid Lanes Ku Lee T'sun, owned by Mrs. C. W. Austin, sired by Ch. Orchid Lane's Ku Lee out of Oberon's Judy of Orchard Hill.

Int. Ch. Calartha Yen Lo of Sualane, owned by Mrs. Gerald Livingston.

Ch. Khi Ku's Ah Bou of Tien Hia, owned by Edith Moorehead.

Langan Nu Tong, owned by Ruby T. Williams.

Ch. Mar Chin Khi Ku's Kopi, owned by Mary McEachin.

in 1961, Apache was turned over to me. They sire quality dogs which can win, but down here we need buyers for our good pekes! It is deplorable that some breeders advertise puppies for $45 up."

This is more than deplorable. How can any one properly feed a puppy to a salable age for such give-away prices! Whole milk, eggs, meat and care, plus inoculation, will cost a lot more than $50 even to raise a healthy pet.

Mrs. C. M. Bateman owns the Ho Ti kennels in Pensacola. She has been raising dogs of the best English and American bloodlines for many years, has Orchard Hill in some pedigrees and owns a granddaughter of Ch. Ku Lee's.

There are many young and enthusiastic new breeders in Texas such as Edith Moorehead. She lives in Houston and has Tien Hia stock, including Ch. Khi Ku's Ah Bou by Ch. Caversham Khi Ku of Pendarvis, which she showed to his title while still a puppy. She also owns Ch. Ping Yangs Griselda of Coughton and Mathena bloodlines. Mrs. Moorehead has been very successful in the few years she has been showing.

Another new kennel owned by Mary McEachin is also founded on Tien Hia stock and in one month of showing she made Mar Chin Khi Ku's Kopi a champion, the tenth champion sired by Khi Ku of Pendarvis.

The William Kidds also of Houston have Ch. Khi Ku's Goblin of Tien Hia. In fact, he was the first Pekingese champion finished by a Houstonian in well over a decade. Mrs. Alice B. Holmes wrote me she had been in Pekes since 1958, that her first dog came from Cornwall and since then, she has had a failing for all things Cornish, so she named her kennel "Quilkin," an ancient name meaning "frog." Mrs. Holmes owns the lovely red import, Ch. Etive Ching of Pinna. He finished with three majors and a group first. She also imported Etive Happy Knight of champion quality, but unfortunately for all concerned he lost an eye several days before his American debut. Bloodlines at "Quilkin" are Alderbourne, Caversham, Sing Lee, Orchard Hill and a "dab" of Kyratown.

Mrs. Ruby Turner Williams has done very well with her He Lo dogs as after only three years of serious breeding she campaigned her first homebred to his title, Ch. Khi Ku's Jin Jin of He Lo. He is by Wee Star Quest of Pekeholme, previously owned by Muriel Freyman. Jin's dam is Khi Ku's Babee of Tien Hia. Another champion at He Lo is a very good black, Sonni Boi's Spankey of Po Yen. Blacks are so necessary in our pedigrees; they keep our colors strong and give us good black masks. He represents line breeding from Int. Ch. Caversham Muh Yin of Mathena.

Horace Wilhoite has a fine kennel in Montgomery, Alabama, founded on Caversham, Alderbourne, Kaytocli and Cho Sen bloodlines. He owns six champions now, with many more soon to gain their titles. His Ch. St. Aubrey Ku Randy is one of Int. Ch. Chik T'sun's best sons. Randy's dam is Ch. Helenes Goblin Surprise, a beautiful import, shown here a few days before whelping. Randy's pedigree is interesting to me as he is a grandson of my Ch. Kai Lung and his granddam Ch. Simba Salote goes back to my famous miniature, specialty and Garden winner, Ch. Pier Simba of Orchard Hill.

Mr. Wilhoite also knows that good blacks are important in our breeding programs. He has Ch. Helenes Black Diamond at stud and owns the black bitch, Ch. Ir Ma Mi Luv Li Black Sprite evidently from Irene Miles' Kennel. He recently acquired an interesting white male, Hallmarks Mr. Checkers which he says is champion quality. He is by Int. Ch. Chick Tu of Peperstiche out of Sheraton Kim of Alderbourne. The expert toy handlers, Clara Alford and Pat Norwood have shown the Helene dogs extensively. Mr. Wilhoite likes to show his own dogs, but being an active businessman he is not able to attend distant shows.

Mr. and Mrs. Paul Ausman have established the Pa We Ja Kennel in Birmingham and had a grand run of wins with one of their first homebreds, Ch. Pa We Ja's Ku Kan Jin. He finished while still a puppy and is shown here winning a group at ten months of age, a dog anyone would be proud to own. His sire is Ch. Jamestown Kai Jin of Caversham out of Pa We Ja's Wei Tina. Mr. Ausman said Tina's background was Orchard Hill down from Ch. Foo Dean and Ch. Bonraye Fo Yu.

Mr. and Mrs. Sam Magun of Albuquerque have raised show dogs since 1957. Their "Peke A Toi" foundation consisted of a show bitch from here followed by Tien Hia and Sing Lee bloodlines meaning Caversham and Alderbourne. Their top champion now is Ah Mee Sing Lee, and soon to finish is Peke A Toi's Peacock by Ch. Chik T'sun of Tien Hia.

Older kennels in Ohio include Mrs. Irene Miles Ir-Ma-Mi Pe-

Ch. Helenes Goblin Surprise, owned by Horace G. Wilhoite.

Ch. Pa We Ja's Ku Kan Jin, bred and owned by Mr. & Mrs. Paul Ausman, shown by Edna Voyles.

Ch. Mu Yin's Son Ni Boi of Po Yen, by Int. Ch. Caversham Moh Yin of Mathena, owned by Wanda Brown.

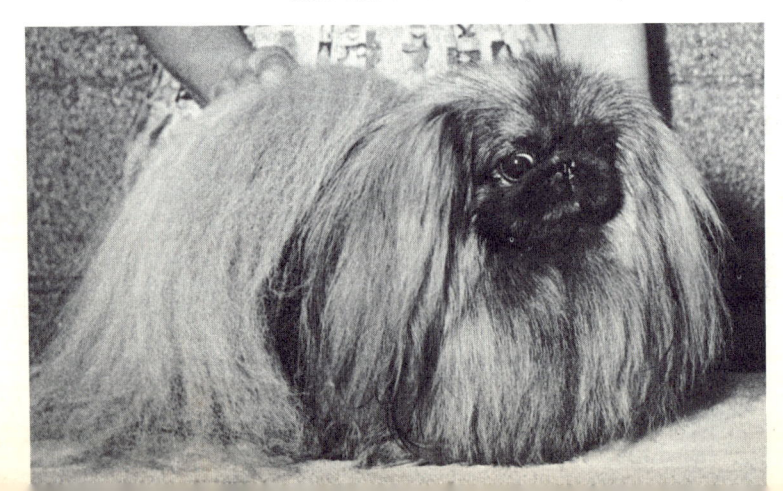

Int. Ch. Ir Ma Mi Ten Mits I Lou Ting, bred and owned by Irene Miles. The only black American bred female to be a Canadian as well as American champion.

Ch. El Acre Me Go Tu, bred by Vivian Longacre. Shown winning Best of Winners at PCA Specialty under noted English judge, Mrs. Donald Wilson, shown by Burton Andrew.

Ch. Audriannes Wei Star.

Ch. Linsown Jon T'sun, owned by Miss Kitty Duff, sired by Ch. Linsown Ku Che Pet.

kingese of Mansfield, Ohio. Of late years, Mrs. Miles has been particularly interested in color breeding, blacks constituting her special endeavor. She had great success in color breeding and her black champions were well known in Midwest competition. Some years ago, Mrs. Miles' kennel and many of her beloved dogs were destroyed by fire, indeed a heart rending experience that shattered her nerves for a time. Gamely, she rebuilt her kennels and was able to restock them, as a few of her best producers were in the house at the time of the fire. She has a black champion at stud, also a black champion bitch, as well as title holders of other colors. She made a grand comeback after her devastating loss. I am glad to report one of her 1964 champions is by our Ch. Nia Sing Tsu Jolity, namely Ir Ma Mi Jee Jol Tum Tum.

Mrs. Vivian Longacre has been breeding and showing champions and selling winners since 1936. Dogs from "El Acre" are noted for profuse coats and correct body conformation. One I particularly liked was her blonde El Acre Ch. Che Fon, a Best-in-Show winner. As I remember it, some of her best stock went back to Ch. Fernway Diamond and Ch. Fernway Golden Oriola. Chefon, bred to a Jalna Hanlin bitch, produced her, Ch. Al Acre K'Buse. Mrs. Longacre wrote, "Most of my stock is old-time Jalna with quite a lot of Ch. Jai Son. Ch. El Acre Sea Foam was to have been a combination of this line breeding. His death was a great loss indeed. He was the only living white American-bred champion of his day. About thirty-odd dogs from El Acre breeding gained their titles." Mrs. Longacre is a "stickler" for soundness and is a well known breeder-judge.

Miss Audrey Atherton has been breeding show dogs for years—more years than one could guess from looking at this young lady! Her good bitch, Ch. Audriannes Wei Star by Ch. Wei Tiko of Pekeboro and her Ch. Cho Sen Fo Lisa did a lot of winning for her. She says she has champion show prospects now sired by Ch. Bettina's Kow Kow. Audrey lives with her parents who are in the prospect of building a $15,000 wing to their new home in Mentor, a "house style" addition making it easier to care for the "Audrianne" dogs. Another successful kennel in Ohio, is "Goodnor," owned by Burton Andrew and Frank Pietrocini of Cleveland. They have El Acre stock and had a grand best of winners at our 1962 specialty with Ch. El Acre Me Go Tu under the noted English judge Mrs. Donald Wilson of Wanstrow fame.

Int. Ch. St. Aubrey Jin T'sun of Holmvallee with two of his daughters, owned by Charleen Prescott.

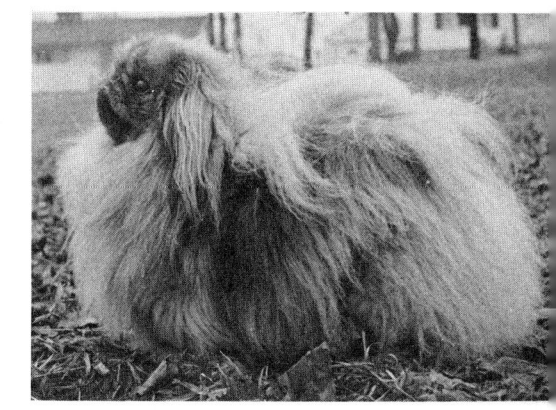

Ch. Popa's Hi Jo, bred & owned by Mrs. Jean Popa.

Miss Prescott with three of her white Pekingese.

Newer Ohio breeders include Mr. and Mrs. Theodore Popa who have done very well and own several champions including Ch. Popa's Hi Jo, a cobby, well balanced homebred plus others being shown which should soon finish.

Miss Kitty Duff of Bridgeport, Ohio, while not an active breeder, is very active in the show ring. Dr. Nancy Lenfestey handled three of her dogs to their titles during the past few years. One came from the Marchessa Maria Bourbon del Monte's lovely place near Como, Italy. His name is Saracene Di Capalbio; the others are Ch. Dragon Pekes Wu Tip, a particolor bitch, then the very good red, Ch. Linsown Jon T'sun by Ch. Linsown Ku Che Pet from Mrs. Pownell's English Kennel.

The Presleen Kennel owned by Charleen Prescott was established in 1959. Their first champion at stud was Ch. Kai Lung Tony by my Ch. Kai Lung of Vinedeans. At that time, the Prescotts also bought a daughter of Ch. Tul Ku Zac of Orchard Hill, of Alderbourne and Caversham breeding, and Holly, a daughter of Ch. Nia Sing Tsu Jolity out of Ch. Poppy of Vinedeans. They have been real producers and prolific ones for Presleen, especially when bred to their Int. Ch. St. Aubrey Jin T'sun of Holmvallee. Their daughters are shown here with him. In less than ten years, the Presleen Kennel piled up an amazing record of Best-in-Show wins, plus many groups wins with Jin T'sun and Ku Mandy. They have been shown fearlessly here and in Canada. Charleen is also very much interested in breeding whites of top show quality. She has at stud Presleen "Snow Twist," a small type white, with correct coat texture. Her other white stud is Langridge Tul Top Notch, imported by Irene Francisco. Miss Prescott is shown here with a litter of whites. The basic aim at Presleen is to raise even better quality and to keep the kennel small, weeding out all but top specimens. Their bitches represent Alderbourne, Caversham, Langridge, Orchard Hill, etc.

Catherine Hendershot is well known in show circles, not only as a serious breeder with many years of experience behind her, but as the owner of that little heart charmer, Luv Li Winkie Poo. He is a beautiful four-pound miniature, a particolor, by another famous little one, Int. Ch. Chik Tu of Peperstiche. Mrs. Henderson owns his dam, Ch. Tul Tana of Alderbourne. Little Winkie Poo is the sire of three champion bitches *in one litter!*

Park Manor, an old and well known name in Chicago, was owned by Ed and Stella Solecki. They bred Pekingese for many years and showed champions in all sections of the country. When they gave up active breeding, Stella became a popular handler and won innumerable titles for her clients. The old established "Lorings" since 1927 are still going strong and still making international champions. Mrs. Ann Loring Lind is shown here, with Mr. and Mrs. Robert Jackson and their three champions, Hi Oasis of Browns Den in the center, his son, Int. Ch. Mr. Frosty of Loring and Int. Champion Desert Gold of Loring, his daughter, bred and owned by the Linds. Ch. Hi Oasis was bred by Cora Brown of California, but is owned by Mrs. Robert Jackson, and was shown extensively by Robert Jackson for their Four Winds Kennel of Seneca. The Jacksons got off to an enviable start years ago, with Fei Sal Lui from here as their first stud and an Orchard Hill champion as matron. In short order, they made a fine show record, and by adding complementary bloodlines they continued to breed winners. Their Hi Oasis was the top American Pekingese sire for 1961 and top sire in United States for 1962. They recently added more Caversham blood through a lovely son of Ch. Caversham Khi Ku of Pendarvis, Ch. Khi Yuki Ku of Wei Toi.

Edward Jenner, of Libertyville became interested in Pekingese and formed a partnership with the popular handler, Mrs. Elaine Rigden, who handles and grooms Pekes to perfection. They bought Ch. Temple Bells of Blossom Lea and have won with him in the East and all through the Midwest. A compact, lovely red he was bred by Jean Grant in her Canadian Blossom Lea Kennel. They have also campaigned extensively the English import, Ch. Ku Jin T'sun of Chintoi. He is by Ku Jin of Caversham and was bred by Ella Page. Jin T'sun is an impressive, profusely coated dog excelling in head points and also shows well. He too has won many groups.

Mrs. Olive N. Nelson, of Waukegan does not show, but has been breeding champion quality dogs for some time. She has other breeds, but her real heart-throbs are of course Pekingese. Her foundation stock is from here, including Caversham, Marglo, Four Winds, and her stud Jai Atom Jan is line-bred Ch. Jai Son Fu out of Golden Girl by Ch. Jai Son by Ch. Jai Son Fu—forty champions directly back of "Jan," an example showing perfect line breeding.

The R. B. Porters have Orchard Hill and Ir Ma Mi as foundation stock, going back to Jai Son and Ch. Pier Simba. Their kennel is located near Stronghurst.

There is an up-and-coming new kennel in Indianapolis called in part for the owners, "Chances R." Mrs. Edna Voyles sent me a picture of one of their champions, the lovely and aptly named, Cho Sen Mei Fly Hyer! That is surely "Chinesey" in name and fly high he did by finishing in a blaze of glory at the Wheaton show. He is owned by Mr. and Mrs. Marion Chance and from his name evidently bred by the Voyles. The Chances will have more champions as another one that finished is their Kan Jin of Caversham sired by Ch. Jamestown Kan Jin of Caversham.

The Mogene Kennel, operated by Mr. and Mrs. Benton Dudgeon of Terre Haute, has done very well since founded a few years ago. One of their top studs is Ch. Mogenes Wi Ja Stu Bai Li. Outstanding show stock here combine Caversham Jehol bloodlines. Mr. and Mrs. Dudgeon, besides raising Pekes and Shih Tzu, have been teaching for many years and have their Masters degrees.

There is an interesting kennel, new to me, in Grand Rapids, the Engstrom's Pekingese, owned by Fred and Anna of that name. They have Caversham and Pekeholme bloodlines and should do very well with that combination.

Vernon L. Lorenzen of St. Paul established his small kennel of show dogs in 1964 with Ch. Ku Lee's Tulya of Orchard Hill. He understands the importance of line breeding and for that purpose he selected Ku Lee Candy from here. He is breeding Tulya to his half-sister, Candy, whose sire is also Ch. Orchid Lanes Ku Lee. Candy's dam Ch. Nia Ku Norma is by Ch. Nia Jai Niki. Norma's dam and Tulya's dam are complementary Alderbourne and Caversham bloodlines. Future champions will surely come from *that* combination.

Going back many years, I must mention the fabulous kennels founded by Mrs. Ralph Boalt of Winona, Wisconsin. From me she bought her first show dog, a lovely small bitch named Blossom. Mrs. Boalt had been ill, so Mr. Boalt phoned me asking about a good bitch as a surprise gift for her. I shipped Blossom to him next day to Daytona Beach, Florida where they were spending the winter for her recovery. As a new interest for Mrs. Boalt I suggested exhibiting Blossom at nearby Florida shows. Never having exhibited before they needed a handler whom they secured in Mrs. Sadie Edmiston.

Ch. Hi Oasis of Browns Den in center. Ch. Lindys Desert Sand of Loring, his daughter, at left, and son, Ch. Lindys Mr. Frosty. Shown with them: Mrs. Jackson, owner of Oasis, Mr. Jackson, Mrs. Ann Lind with her Frosty, Judge Mrs. Marie Meyer.

Ch. Cho Sen Mei Fly Hyer, owned by Mr. & Mrs. Marion Chance.

Ch. Tulya of Orchard Hill, owned by Vernon Lorenzen.

Ch. Temple Bells of Blossomlea, owned by Elaine Rigdon and Edward Jenner.

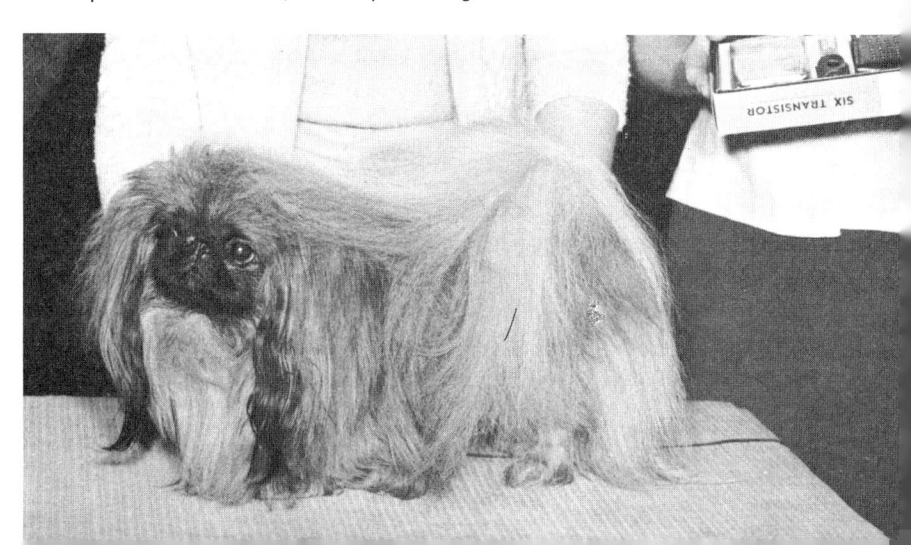

Blossom was shown shortly afterward at Tampa where, handled by Mrs. Edmiston, she won best of breed and best toy. Now comes the real interesting part of the story which proves what can happen to a novice! Mrs. Edmiston had contracted to show a client's Chow that had won the non-sporting group, so Mrs. Boalt was forced to show her own Peke in the finals. You've guessed it—she beat Mrs. Edmiston's Chow and, at what was Blossom's first, and Mrs. Boalt's first show as well, she took the top award of Best in Show all breeds, winning five points on her title! Needless to say, Peach Blossom of Orchard Hill was soon a champion.

After this terrific start, Mariel Boalt became really interested. On their way North, Mr. and Mrs. King and their charming daughter stopped at Orchard Hill and purchased several show bitches. They tried to talk me into selling my new sensation, Tri-Int. Ch. Pierrot of Hartlebury and Ch. Humming Bee of Alderbourne's beautiful daughter, Ch. Princess Picotee. Later on, Picotee won Morris and Essex under Mrs. Mathis and was also a Pekingese Club champion. Mrs. King's flattering offers tempted me, but I was firm and refused to sell. As things turned out my guardian angel must have been close that day. I kept Pierrot here. He went on to become a world-famous champion and Best in Show winner, one of the really great sires of all time. Since Pierrot was not for sale, and since Mrs. Boalt wanted only the best, she invited Mrs. Edmiston to go abroad with her. After a tour of English kennels they came home with some of England's best including Ch. Liebling of Huntington and Ch. Woo Fu of Kingswere, an outstanding dog, a champion well remembered for his great show record as well as for his regal bearing and wonderful type. Ill health continued to plague Mrs. Boalt, who finally had to give up. Her dogs were sold to Mr. Maytag and shown several years longer under the Ceylon Court colors and Maytag ownership. A young handler in those days, Ruth Burnett had charge of the show dogs and won a great deal for Mrs. Boalt and later for Maytag. Known today as Mrs. Ruth Sayres and associated more closely with Poodles, Ruth's first big wins were made with Pekes. Her special favorite was Liebling, one of the most beautiful bitches I ever saw and one that we all wanted to own.

But to return to Mrs. Boalt. Before leaving "dear Mariel," I must tell something that quite impressed me at the time. One evening she phoned me from Winona, Wisconsin, that she was driving to

Ch. Phaletas Wa Net, 5½ lb. miniature, bred and owned by Hazelle Ferguson.

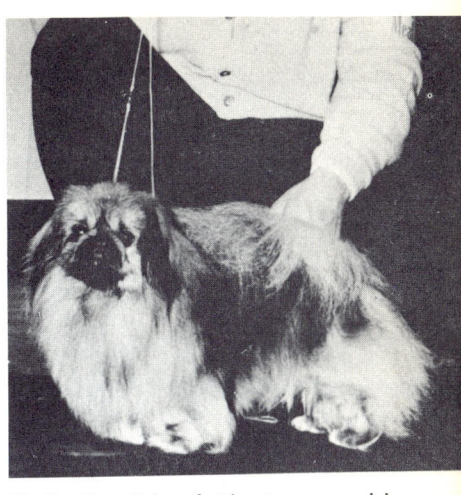

Ch. Ken-Yons-Eicho of Atherstone, owned by Mrs. Walter Brant, bred by George Davidson.

Townsend Trophy, J. P. Morgan Cup, other important trophies. Ch. Fei Jai Son in cup.

Lock Haven since she wanted me to look at Blossom's feet! Coming halfway across the continent, she spent a memorable weekend with us, just to have Blossom's toe nails cut! I will never forget her arrival. She had just returned from Paris with a very becoming hairdo, and *red* painted fingernails, the first I had ever seen. Her nails matched a new Rolls Royce, a lush special body convertible. She and Blossom made an effective picture as her chauffeur in snappy French uniform escorted them to our door and a welcome on the terrace. The last time I saw Mariel was an accidental meeting in Key West. We spent the afternoon talking over old times, old friends and the dogs she had loved. Mariel was in Florida for the same reason we were—on a fishing trip after that hard-to-catch, fast running bonefish. We had caught some big ones off the Keys near Marathon. We told her about a certain Captain Harry Snow and some of our favorite fishing flats. This meeting plus Christmas cards and an occasional letter from Hawaii where Mariel is now living marks a fascinating episode in my Pekingese past.

I could continue to reminisce sadly over friends who are no longer here, who so loyally supported Pekingese and made showing, winning, or losing a matter of fun and good sportsmanship.

One of those lovable Pekingese supporters was the late William Breed and his mother. They upheld the Cleveland Classic in its darkest days and made it *the* show of the Midwest. Their own Pekingese kennel was a small one; their dogs took turns as house pets and no favorites played. I remember their special interest was in particolors with which they did their share of winning. Bill Breed and his column in *Popular Dogs*, "The Little Black Bag" will surely be recalled and generous Bill was loved by all who knew him. The Cleveland Classic remains a monument to him. In my own home I have a memorial to him, the fabulous Townsend Trophy, not for winning the air races at Cleveland, but for many years of exhibiting dogs there and of eventually being the lucky winner of this magnificent trophy. Through Bill Breed's solicitation the Townsend family offered this trophy for the toy group winner to be won five times. The cup was purchased in London at the Christy auction sale when the famous Kaiser Wilhelm's silver collection was dispersed. It is an early Augsberg Sacristy piece for sacred wine, an altar piece quite priceless now.

I believe there are more breeders in California and on the Coast than in any section of the country. I am sorry I cannot review all of them. Early breeders who helped make Pekingese history of the West were Lydia Hopkins and her Sherwood winners, Mrs. W. A. Martel with Ashcroft importations, Mrs. Eugenia Kelly, Mrs. Hortense Blakesley and her Ch. Pierrot son, Mrs. Marjorie Nye Phulps and her interest in breeding blacks. In fact, I believe she founded her kennel on a mating to my Ch. S. As. Hanshih and from that breeding obtained her Ch. Japeke Hamshihs Domino. She also secured the same bloodlines and more blacks by breeding the same bitch to Mrs. Sears' Ch. Rajah of Hesketh. She was one of the pioneer breeders of blacks in this country. Color breeding requires years of pedigree study and should not be attempted unless one is very young and has plenty of money to spend on *known* producers of pure whites or all blacks.

Other early kennels of note are the Pekelands owned by Mrs. Butler, Mrs. Sidell and the Caro Dels. George Bindley Davidson inherited his love for Pekingese from his mother who founded the well known "Atherstone" kennels. She was one of our great pioneer breeders and since her death Mr. Davidson has carried on the strain and continues to breed Atherstone winners. The old established Pekwell Kennels "Home of Champions," the well known Dorristers, Margaret Carey and her champions, one being Kung Chu Hey Yen of Atherstone which achieved this feat at a young eight years! Later, came Mrs. Smith and her family from England. They brought Alderbourne stock and established the Langridge Kennels and in a short time bred and sold many champions. Ch. Landridge New Tong was their biggest winner and Wee Maid of Elfann, their best producing dam. After Mrs. Smith's death, her daughter, Mrs. Irene Smith Francisco, imported more dogs personally selected by her in England and still continued to breed winners. Their kennel now is mainly a stud kennel with Etive Ming, a son of Chinaman of Alderbourne to carry on the line.

Mrs. Neva McMunn did a lot of winning with her Pierrot and Jai Son stock and is still breeding quality dogs with the added Ch. Thomas Tombo line. Mrs. Inez Graf bred champions from her imports and does her share of winning. Mrs. Hazelle Ferguson sent me an outline of her kennel which is especially interesting to me, as she says her first bitch was a daughter of Ch. Pier Halle of Orchard Hill afterwards bred to Ch. Cha Ming Boi Pierrot. Mrs. Ferguson's first champion was Gay Tune, all Orchard Hill and her full sister Ch. Shelan Phaleta, her second champion produced Ch. Cassa Lana. Six champions came from those bloodlines. Mrs. Ferguson keeps only three bitches to breed and wrote, "In all my experience, I have had only one litter that failed to produce a champion." Quite a record I would say. She has made seventeen champions, two also are Mexican champions. A star there is the lovely five and one-half pound miniature, Ch. Wa Ne'T, a consistent winner, shown twenty-two times with twenty-one wins. She won both specialties and needs only one more show to be a Mexican International champion. Ch. T'an Wo is Wa Ne'ts litter brother jointly owned by Mrs. Ferguson's sister-in-law and Mrs. Vera Croften, made the seven Texas fall shows, and went best toy at all seven!

Shirley Stone has been very successful with her Chun Chu Fu dogs for a long time and is also a handler and shows in all parts of the country, even East and Ohio. I know she has bred many champions, but do not know the exact number. She has sent bitches to many prominent studs such as Ch. Calartha Manderin, Ch. Chik T'sun, etc. So her dogs combine nearly all the winning bloodlines. Two of her favorite champions are the very good females, Ch. Melodee and the one pictured here, Ch. Katrina.

Ruth and Irving Livingston have been in Pekes for twenty-seven years and have had many thrilling wins. One of the first "greats" was Ch. Meiling Ku Bee by Ch. Ku Chi of Caversham; he sired four champions for them. Their other imports were Ch. Ravenswood Pei King of Samurai, Ch. Coughton Ping T'sun followed by three Copplestone champions, twelve of their dogs gaining championship honors. Their past two winners are Ch. Copplestone Puma of Jenntora and his brother, Ch. Copplestone Pulle. The Livingstons do not have a kennel now, due to ill health, but they still show. The dogs they have now are like children to them and are house pets.

Elsie Love Jones and her Bantam Ranch dogs are a legend. She, too, has cut down to a few house pets. We still get her cheerful letters and her wonderful Christmas poems.

In 1957, a new star rose in the West. Mrs. Vera Crofton became interested in Pekingese and put "Monte Verde" on the map. I have no figures on how many champions she imported through Nigel Jones and William Taylor or the number of champions bred from them. They were campaigned not only in Canada but all over the

Ch. Katrina, breeder-owner Shirley Stone.

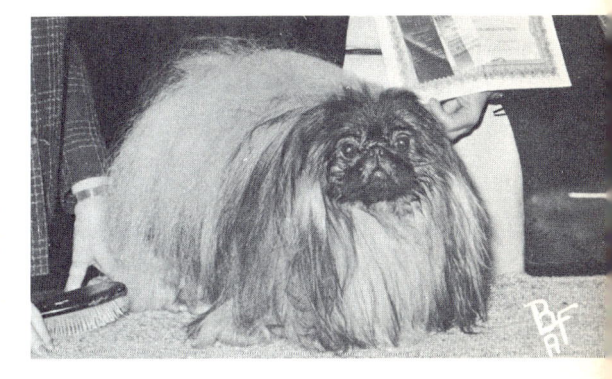

Ch. Copplestone Puma of Jenntora, by Ch. Copplestone Pu Zee, owners Mr. & Mrs. Livingston.

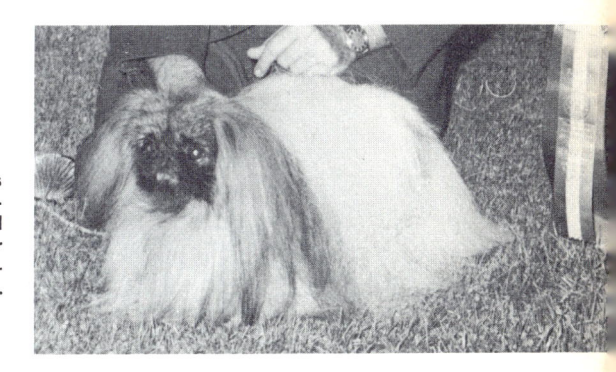

Ch. Mar Pat Tiko's Tom Thumb. Top winning American bred for 1962. Breeder owners, Martha Bingham & Pat Miller.

Ch. Chui Mong Dai, owned by Donna E. Creley, Esther Yeager.

States. Those I have seen and admired are the three English "greats." Tri-Int. Ch. Calartha Mandarin of Jehol, made his title as a youngster in England, then piled up group and Best-in-Show wins in Canada. Then later, under Monte Verde colors, he was shown by Frank Sabella winning Best in Show seven times plus thirty-seven group wins. The second dog is Int. Ch. Rikki of Calartha, a Mandarin son; third, a Mandarin grandson, Ch. St. Aubrey Seminole of Wanstrow. His wins include four times Best in Show, and twice best of breed at coast specialty shows and eleven group firsts. Also at Monte Verde is Ch. St. Aubrey Yung Derrie of Soozan. He was best of breed at Westminster in 1962. When Mrs. Crofton came East for this event in 1963, she was well rewarded by seeing her Ch. St. Aubrey Siminole win the breed over five well known champions including her own young Ch. St. Aubrey Bo T'sun of Elsdon. Bo T'sun died suddenly while being shown that spring.

It is interesting to note, especially for new breeders that "stamina," if that is the proper word, is tougher in some dogs than others, such as in Jai Son. He won best of breed at our P.C.A. specialty at a young nine years of age and following that theory as I write this, Ch. Calartha Mandarin, in my opinion, is still top man at Monte Verde. Mrs. Crofton moved her dogs to Montreal where her nine champions are at stud. Ch. St. Aubrey Tinka Belle, best of breed at our summer specialty, is a Mandarin daughter.

The Mar Pat Kennels owned by the sisters, Martha Bingham and Patricia Miller, have made a terrific record since they began in 1953. They house about thirty dogs of which Ch. Tiko of Pekeboro reigns supreme and no wonder! Imported in 1956, he completed his title in two months and then sired eight champions, and is grand sire of six. Fifteen champions have been bred so far at Mar Pat, of which two are Best-in-Show dogs. The top winner retained in the kennel is Ch. Mar Pat Tiko's Tom Thumb, with many groups to his credit, Best-in-Show wins, and best of breed at specialties. He was top winning American-bred for 1962 and is sired by Ch. Tiko. Dam is Sun 'T Glory Sing Lee, the dam of three champions. Mar Pat is also very proud of another lovely homebred champion, their Ch. Mar Pat Mandarin's Star. She is out of their Ch. Mar Pat Jade.

Mrs. Cora Brown had a choice small kennel including six champions. Two of them, Ch. Oasis of Browns Den and Ch. Hi Oasis are owned and were shown to their titles by the Jacksons of "Four

Winds." Ch. Hi Oasis, sire of eight champions, was 1962 top sire in the United States. Since the death of her husband and her own ill health, Mrs. Brown has reduced her stock but still has several champions at stud and a few good litters coming on.

Donna Creley with co-owner Esther Yeager did a lot of winning with their Ch. Chui Mong Doi Don Ho, a lovely homebred, a grandson of Ch. Major Mite of Honan. The Bergums, Elaine and William, are breeding top show dogs these days and one that I especially admire and would like to own is pictured here, the small red male Ch. Ko Ko Puff of Ber Gum. Note his perfect head, tail set, and well balanced body. A credit to his sire, Ch. Mandarin and his dam, Ch. Yung Lin Tu of Ber Gum. Elaine also bred the very good bitch, Ch. Sun Tuling of Bergum. She says of her, "The best bitch we have bred so far, won five points at the Arizona specialty under Hazelle Ferguson."

Mrs. Lois Frank had some grand wins with her Ch. Sunny Boy of Tien Hia, a beautiful son of the late Ch. Khi Ku of Pendarvis. She handled him to the title and is pictured here winning a strong Toy group at Victoria, Canada. "Sunny" was bred by Lola Broods.

New breeders on the Coast are numerous, such as that well informed young man, Harry Aldrich of Chico. He has studied pedigrees and line breeding, has learned fast and has established a fine kennel of show stock headed by his first champion, Ku Chi T'Jai Mi of Orchard Hill. He bought him just after he won best puppy at our Westchester specialty. Now Harry has a real feather in his cap. Ch. Ku Chin Tom Mi of Seng Kye, bred at his kennel, is now a sensational winner. At seven and one-half months he was best of winners at the Coast specialty, then took a strong group at Ventura at nine months, finished at ten months, and won the Del Monte group at thirteen months! Irene Rauchhaupt saw him, bought him, and made him a famous young champion. Now off to a good start in 1964, he won best of breed at the big Golden Gate specialty. Famous winners are not new to Mrs. Ruschhaupt; she is one of our best known breeders and has made at least fifty champions for her Sing Lee Kennels. She was fortunate indeed when she bought Thelma Pollar's lovely import Shan Ling Little Puff. He quickly gained his title, won the Pacific Coast specialty and sired Int. Ch. Shan Ling Sing Lee, the top winning Pekingese in the States in 1956 with 3566 points. He was the top winning toy dog in California

Ch. Ko Ko Puff of Ber Gum, breeder owner Elaine Bergum.

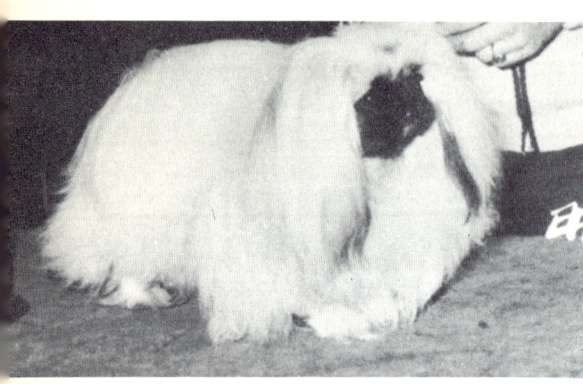

Ch. Mr. Peepers of Browns Den, bred & owned by Cora Brown.

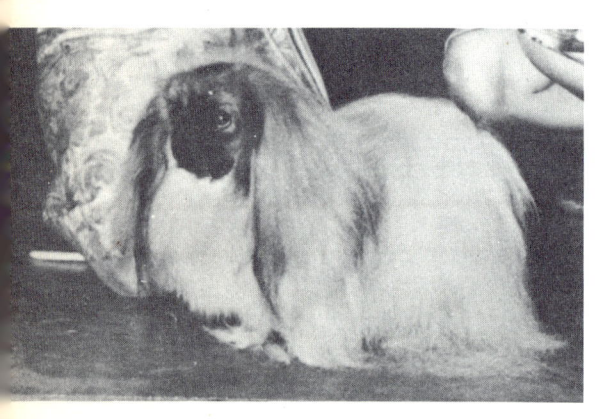

Ch. Sunny Boy of Tien Hia, owned by Mrs. Frank.

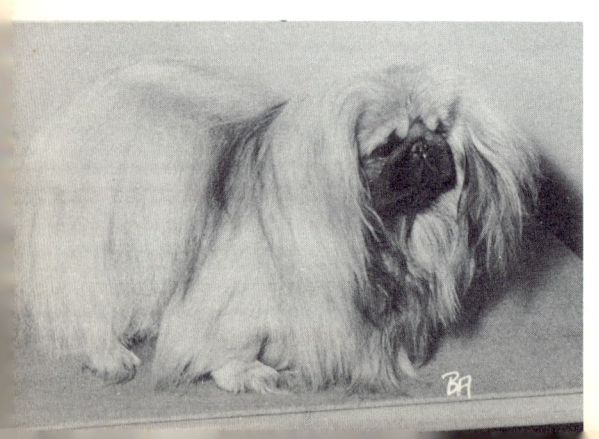

Ch. Ku Chi Jai Mi of Orchard Hill, owner Harry Aldrich.

that year and won the largest Pekingese show, and was fourth winning toy dog all in one year. He sired Tri-Int. Ch. Ditto Shan Sing Lee.

Another successful breeder is Marvel Runkel of Spokane. She did very well with Roh Kai champions and is now winning groups with Int. Ch. St. Aubrey Perri of Wellplace. Mrs. McCann had nice wins with her good black-and-tan Ch. Pat Tez Tam Mei, and has stock from my Ch. Kai Lung, in fact, she sent a very good Krieger bitch, here, back in 1956 and from that mating came five females, and the founding of her kennel. She is also interested in obedience training. Seven of her dogs have C.D. degrees and one has his C.D.X. Mrs. McCann bought half interest in Marvel Runkel's Ch. St. Aubrey Argus of Wellplace, being shown in both names. At this writing his wins include Best in Show four times and nineteen group firsts!

Another great winner of the Northwest is Int. Ch. Kee Ting China's Toni, bred and owned by Carita Grieve. Her Kee Ting Kennels are in British Columbia, Canada. His record is amazing—shown thirty-four times, best of breed thirty-three times, then thirty-one groups, ten times Best in Show, and chosen to represent the standard for Western Canada. His dam, Ch. Ro Ge's China Girl was bred by Rose Wilmarth of Seattle. Mrs. Grieve wrote, "Gene Hahnlin has shown Toni to all his wonderful wins; they are a hard team to beat."

Another up-and-coming new kennel of the Northwest is owned by Lloyd Stacy of Tacoma. He sent me the following data: "After the purchase of Ch. Roh Kai Genie's Ching Jen in late 1959, I took him to Canada and made him an Int. Ch. He won the group in nearly every Canadian show he was in, and had the grand win of Best in Show at Edmonton. Then, I imported Alderbourne Fair Lady of Shirley Moor and showed her to American championship. I also own Int. Ch. St. Aubrey Perri of Elsdon. He finished at the Chicago International and has been doing a fine job of taking the groups since then." Mr. Stacy will campaign another fine import to the title, his Alderbourne Ogle of Coughton. He has bred Ch. Fair Lady to him and expects something really great from that combination.

Years ago, when I judged the Seattle specialty show, I met Mr. and Mrs. Frank Creasey of Vancouver and judged some of their fine

Ch. Ku Chin Tom Mi of Seng Kye, owner Irene Ruschhaupt, winning central Calif. specialty. Note trophy won, carved teakwood Fu dogs.

Int. Ch. Kee Ting China's Toni, bred-owned by Carita Grieve, Saanichtok, B.C., Can., sired by Ch. Etive Helenes Twee Jin.

Int. Ch. St. Aubrey Argus of Wellplace, co-owners Marvel Runkle & Mrs. F. R. McCann.

Car O Del Pekes. I asked him, "Where do you get such coats?" His reply is just as important today as it was years ago. "I am a firm believer that coats must be bred and cannot be created to any successful degree. By the same token, I have so often seen coats *being the cause* of a dog going up, that it sometimes makes me wonder whether a good coat on a poor dog is not a detriment to the breed. Too many judges allow their eye to influence their judgment, when their hands should be detecting the hidden faults so often found under that glamorous covering." Mr. Creasey sent me a picture of their black Int. Champion in 1952. He compares most favorably with our best blacks of today. Their Ch. H'in San of Car O Del was the top sire of his day. His progeny accounted for forty-four group firsts, sixteen Best-in-Show wins and twenty-three best Canadian-bred in show.

Mrs. Grace Krieger and her Marglo Kennels at Lynnwood are known all over the country. She is noted for her homebred champions which did so well for her on the Coast and up into Canada. Mrs. Stella Solecki of Chicago exhibited the Krieger dogs fearlessly not alone in that area, but through the Southwest and gained many titles for them. I, myself, campaigned successfully little Ch. Marglo's Bon Yu Kim Toi, best of winners at the 1955 Westminster. Bred by Mrs. Krieger, he was one of the few really top miniature studs on the bench of that time. He sired champions for me and is back of many present day winners. I am proud to say Orchard Hill stock was the foundation of the Marglo Kennels, in fact we find Ch. Jai Son on back to Ch. S. Av Hanshih and Ch. Pierrot in the pedigrees of many West Coast dogs. Mrs. Krieger sent this data to me. "Jai Han Sung was the foundation of my Kennel. He excelled in head points and passed them on through many generations. All my champions are down from him. He had his majors when he lost an eye and could not finish. Combined bloodlines of Jai Son, Ch. Bon Yu Toi and Oberon of Elfann gave us twenty champions. The most recent one is Sum Chik. She is by my Int. Ch. Ku Rah of Elsdon; dam is from my Jai Han Sung line." Mrs. Ralph Lynch had a few Orchard Hill dogs then later with Honan stock, she had nice wins with Ch. Captain Tiny Mite, bred by Mrs. Reynolds.

Mrs. Anna Young, formerly of the Coast, bred champions and consistent winners for a long time and is one of our best known older breeders. She may not be breeding now, but her "Logus Road" dogs

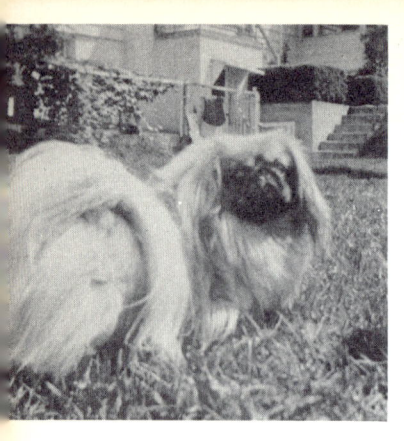

Ch. Helenes Royal Robin of Blossomlea, owned by Mrs. Yan Paul, an import bred by Mrs. H. Choster.

Ch. Ku Rah Sum Chik, bred, owned and shown by Grace Krieger. Judge Trullinger.

Int. Ch. Shan Ling Sing Lee. Top winning Pekingese in 1956. Breeder owner, Irene Ruschhaupt.

Int. Ch. Starlett of Jalna, bred by Zara Smith.

are in many of our pedigrees. Mrs. Young is a popular *breeder*-judge, and how we need them! Here I must mention Mrs. Ione Reynolds, whose astute breeding gave us the famous Ch. Major Mite of Honan. Mrs. MacDonald was another pioneer of the Northwest. She showed many fine winners, some of which date back to my early stock. Lack of further data, and space too, forbids a review of all the kennels of this area. I can write only of the ones best known to me and those specifically who sent me material and pictures.

Northwest Coast and Oregon breeders will remember Dorothy Piazza's winners, such as Ch. Piazza's Peppermint Jeep, Best in Show all breeds at San Francisco's Golden Gate show, Ch. Jeep and lovely Ch. Parfait which did so well for her and for others who bought them when she gave up breeding.

It is hard for me to write about "Jalnas." I have known Zara Smith for years. I believe we have persevered more than many other old kennels to promote and keep our breed in the limelight, trying to keep it the most popular of all toy breeds. Zara Smith bred the one and only Int. Ch. Wee Starlett, a magnificent bitch that I saw in her kennel years ago. She had the distinction of being dam of eight champions and grand dam of fifteen more, and will surely go down in history for this feat, a record I believe for our breed. Starlett died in 1956 at the ripe old age of fourteen. There are at least fifty Jalna bred champions, their progeny producing still more winners for those who have Jalna stock. Mrs. Ann Samet is now joint ownership with Mrs. Smith. She is young and will carry on and keep their colors flying with that outstanding young Ch. Jalnas Kwan On Wing.

Mrs. Eugene Hahnlin and her well known international champions, under the old prefix of Han Lin, are back in many present-day pedigrees. Gene is a popular well known handler and made not only many champions for their own kennels but for others in the Northwest and Canada. He ventured East years ago to our Summer specialty at Morris and Essex, where he was victorious over our top winners and captured best of breed with Int. Ch. Chia Lee Han Lin. I understand that this profusely coated black homebred won seven specialty shows plus several Best-in-Show fixtures, and left champions for them to keep Han Lin a winning kennel then and now.

Homebreds and many imports are keeping things lively on the

Coast. All have won in keenest competition. I am curious to see how their bloodlines will nick. I know they will if new breeders will study pedigrees and have the patience to find out the faults as well as the virtues of every dog in at least a four-generation pedigree.

On up North and as far as I know there is but one Pekingese kennel in Alaska. And here is the strange thing about it—it is mostly Orchard Hill and Alderbourne! Mrs. Charlotte B. Cowell of Fairbanks and Fort Wainwright, the owner, gave me these facts after I wrote her about Alaska show wins. Late in 1959, I sold Chang Ti of Alderbourne and my Sun Fu's Fei Fei to Mrs. C. Dunkin of Puerto Rico. They won there, but dropped from sight until I read of Chang Ti being shown in Alaska. Mrs. Cowell's husband is in the Air Force and evidently bought the dogs for his wife while in Puerto Rico and flew them to Alaska. At the Tanana show, Fei Fei's Pan Su Yen Rojo won her second major and when this is read I hope she will have won her title. She is by Chang Ti and Sun Fu's Fei Fei of Orchard Hill. The Cowells also own Ch. Dae Mus of Sumead, a toy group winner with Ch. Bonraye Fo Yu back of him. Mrs. Cowell wrote, "Pekingese are just getting started in Alaska. I am the only one in Fairbanks who raises them, but I heard of a woman in Anchorage who has a few Pekes from the 'Sing Lee' line." I wrote Mrs. Cowell that I too know of a girl who wants to breed Pekingese in Alaska. Her name is Nancy Ann Nichols of Tok Cut Off near Mentasta. She asked for pedigrees and data of bitches that might be for sale.

Canadian Kennels would make a Volume Two, as England is partly there with the same bloodlines and English stock as in the States. Some older kennels that were established way back in the war days were owned by that delightful, well beloved lady, Mrs. C. de P. Doniphan of Wanza fame. Her letters to me still prove that reciprocity, not borderlines, make us not only neighbors, but one Continent undivided.

Mrs. Yan Paul of Willowdale has bred and line-bred champions, for more years than I know. She also had Chows, but concentrated later on Pekingese. From pedigrees of her older Pekes, one was her winning Ch. Jai Son Shades and as name implies goes back to Jai Son. Mrs. Paul made four champions in 1963—Ch. Kei Ting China's Emperor, Ch. Helenes Robin of Blossom Lea, Ch. Helenes Red Lady and Ch. Kee Ting Aleis Tuen. Mrs. Paul is one of our best known *breeder*-judges.

I do not have Jean Grant's "Blossom Lea" address, but I do know she moved her English dogs to Canada about 1961, and is the proud breeder of Ch. Temple Bells of Blossom Lea, now owned by Elaine Rigden and Edward Jenner.

Mr. and Mrs. R. W. Chalton, near St. Thomas, have a choice small kennel and although they both have important jobs, they hope to raise show puppies from stock they bought here. This also applies to another young couple, the F. W. Huestons, now owners of Nia Ku Chia by "Sailor." Chia won a major in the States, then was retired to raise a litter. Mrs. Mosley, the breeder of Ch. Black Queen of Orchard House, dam of Bettinas Ch. Kow Kow, came here and helped the Huestons select a show bitch and then bought a show male herself. Mrs. Mosley brought her dogs over from England and is now settled in Canada. We wish her good luck and I know she will give us all keen competition.

Now we come to the well known St. Aubrey Elsdon Kennel operated by Nigel Aubrey-Jones and William Taylor. I met Nigel in England when I judged there, then later in 1952 I bought Ch. St. Aubrey Judy of Calartha from him. He was coming to Canada on a business trip and not only brought Judy over for me that September, but Ch. Pu Chi of Perryacre as well. I bought Puchi from Mrs. Allison Rae after he won his first challenge certificate. Judy was entered at our summer specialty show where Nigel showed her to best of winners and her first five points. Incidentally, it was I who introduced him to the Pekingese fancy, to breeders and exhibitors at that show. Nigel handled Judy for me in Canada where she finished in three shows. Then in short order we gained her American title and Judy became the only Tri-International champion bitch of that time. Their Ch. Ku Rah of Elsdon, a Best-in-Show winner by Ch. Chik T'sun, is out of their Simba Salina, by my Ch. Kai Lung and as name indicates, goes way back to our famous miniature Ch. Pier Simba.

Since then many famous dogs have been imported by Jones and Taylor including the one and only Ch. Chik T'sun of Caversham, later sold to the Venables. They also have beautiful homebreds, such as Int. Ch. St. Aubrey Tinkabelle of Elsdon, twice best of breed at our Westchester specialty, and Best in Show at the Progressive Dog Club for all toys. One lovely bitch Nigel owned was little "Rosebud." We all loved her. She was one of the few miniatures to gain top honors. When she died from an accident while still young, Nigel must have felt as badly as we did when Ch. Pier Simba went to join St. Anthony upstairs.

Most of us have seen dogs from the Capalbio Kennels of Como, Italy, owned by the Marchesa M. Luise Bourbon del Monte. Her kennel was founded on the best British bloodlines, carefully chosen for line breeding, such as her Ch. Wei Chik Tu of Peperstiche. The picture of him here was taken at eleven months and shows perfection in head points. Later, when in full coat he won top honors for Capalbio under English as well as Continental judges.

Luz Margarita Lewald Countess Von Roon of Santiago de Chile sent pictures of her three Capalbio champions. One of them, Ch. Basileio di Capalbio, won Best in Show at Santiago. The judge, Dr. Porter Miller, told her "he was the best dog in South America and could win in any competition." The Countess also has an exquisite four-pound miniature, Ch. Geranei di Capalbio. She wrote, "Even though so small he is lion-hearted, afraid of nothing. He once attacked a Collie in my defense."

The popularity of the Pekingese has even spread to Africa. When I was in Nairobi several years ago, I saw four dogs of real show type, and now comes a letter from Mrs. V. M. Siebert, a new breeder, living in Bulawayo, Southern Rhodesia. She wants to breed show dogs and asked for several copies of this book and said, "It is very difficult to obtain breed books in this country. I want to introduce yours to the Pekingese breeders of Rhodesia."

There are too many English kennels to attempt to review them in one volume as they are legion! All Pekingese are founded on British bloodlines; we know their pedigrees and have been line breeding their stock for many years. Most of us know what our studs can do, which ones sire better heads, better legs, shorter bodies, coat, etc. This also applies to our matrons, but we do not use outside studs as much as we should. It is not that way in England. Studs from other kennels are used; one that seems best suited for a certain bitch. Distances in England are shorter than over here, and shipping not as complicated. The dread and risk of shipping long distances in this country may be one of the reasons we do not use outside studs. Perhaps some of us prefer to have our dogs completely home-bred, sire as well as dam. In the long run this may be a mistake as we are liable to inbreed faults. Before we get into *that* rut try a sire of compatible bloodlines owned elsewhere.

Ch. Wei Chik Tu of Peperstiche, owner Marchesa Luisa Bourbon del Monte.

Ch. Basillio di Capalbio, owner Margarita Lewald, Countess von Roon.

Japanese Ch. Chun Chu Fu's Chuck-a-Luck, breeder Shirley Stone, owner Paul Yoshida.

5

Mistakes and Successes

W HAT is it that keeps a breeder hard at work answering all manner of questions from novices? Any number of breeders do this. Perhaps, as some have claimed, it appeals to one's vanity to be asked for advice! If vanity does promote the impulse, then it brings its own special punishment in the labor entailed in trying to hold the beginner to the straight and narrow path of progress.

I do not think vanity enters into the matter at all. Nor can it be called a labor of love exactly, this job of replying to queries ranging all the way from sound to silly. Sometimes, if the truth were told, most of us grow quite exasperated with it, but still we go right on answering to the best of our ability.

The average breeder's desire to help the novice, I think, is rooted in his own pride in the dog of his choice. Having attained a certain measure of success himself, having seen his breed grow year by year in beauty and popularity, naturally he wants his favorite to hold his place in the sun of universal regard. And this is possible only by enticing new recruits constantly into the ranks and of keeping them there until they learn enough of the principles of the game to stick with it as regulars.

Of course there is always considerable difference of opinion about method and management. But on one thing, and perhaps only one, an overwhelming majority agree, and that is the vital importance of the start. The first few years are the hardest; these will indicate clearly whether the novice is going anywhere or not. In fact, there are a number of things which the beginner definitely should and should not do. But were I to lay down the law, so to speak, and say *you must do this,* and *you mustn't do that,* the novice would immediately shy off and take his troubles elsewhere, and they would not be doggy troubles either, for he would have deserted the game almost before he began. Novices can be led; they cannot be driven.

By way of such instruction as I am happy to give, I have already mentioned my own faulty start; I'll go on to tell of its subsequent correction and the principle methods of breeding I used which furnished the groundwork of the progress I made. If newcomers in Pekingese, as well as those who may not be making the progress they think they should, will draw their own conclusions from my experience and really take the lessons to heart, I believe they will have just as much chance as I did to forge ahead without spending too much time about it.

Before they have been breeding very long, they will realize that we never stop learning. We cannot afford to, for always just around the corner is something new cropping up; some new trick of breeding, feeding, kennelling or whatever, which must be understood, its fundamentals grasped, if our knowledge is to keep abreast of the times and our dogs in the forefront of competition.

Only in retrospect can we appreciate the true value of our mistakes. At least this was so in my own case when a breeder, in misrepresenting her dogs, took advantage of my ignorance and foisted worthless stock upon me. This type of salesmanship goes on all the time. Especially where dogs are sold by mail, their good points are often exaggerated, their faults played down or not mentioned. Advertisements may be so adroitly worded as to mislead even the alert buyer regarding the standing and reputation of the kennel. Many a potential breeder becomes disappointed with his first purchase and gives up in disgust; or, what is equally deplorable, he thinks these reprehensible practices are centered in one breed and so decides to interest himself in another.

However, the picture is not all dark by any means, for there are in business today reputable establishments from which the buyer may select good dogs and get his money's worth; just as there are breeders who meticulously explain a puppy's right and wrong characteristics, his virtue and his failings, whatever they may be, and give value for value received.

As I mentioned at the start of this chapter, there are sincerely animated breeders who welcome novice trade and handle it with impeccable technique. What is more, they go to great lengths to start the novice right and to advise him if need be as he goes along. This, in my opinion, is the most vital phase of any kennel's beginning: that the novice seek out a reputable expert, and then rely upon his direction. Such reputable expert may be an old-time breeder, he may be a judge or possibly a professional handler. Whoever it is, if he is the right kind of person, he will be as ready to help others as he is to help himself. And as for the novice, willingness to be guided by the experience of others in the same field is the sole means of getting a head start in this highly competitive hobby of breeding dogs.

I do not spare myself one bit when I confess to more than my share of impatience. Most authors who have written interestingly and well about the various phases of breeding recommend that the beginner start at the bottom with puppies and learn as the little ones grow. Without doubt this is sound advice; I have seen it work out commendably many times. However, that *go slow* halo simply would not fit on my head. I knew my limitations, which is something! I never did like climbing ladders step by step: I knew by that method I would never last long enough to get to the top. So in keeping with my impetuous disposition, I decided to jump for the top and hang on if I could.

Only at this moment do I realize the chance I took, for I see now what I was too ignorant to see then, namely, that if I did not hold on when I had the top in my grasp I would have farther to fall, with humiliation heaped up and overflowing. But that did not bother me. I was typical of all novices who, because they do not know, have more courage than the old-timer who has travelled the course and remembers the pitfalls. What saved me from disaster was that initial lesson I learned: to seek and accept the counsel of the experienced.

The strength of a kennel lies in its matrons my mentor told me. Anyone willing to pay the required fee could breed to any champion stud of suitable bloodlines. The females were the only safe foundation stones upon which to build. So, turning a deaf ear to the voice of the many, I followed without question the words of my chosen teacher. I bought the very finest bitch obtainable, Grey Spider of Hesketh, and soon made her a champion. In less than three years I had five champion bitches including the specialty show winning bitch, and another that was the only bitch in Pekingese history to win championships in four countries.

Only when I had reached this stage did I purchase studs to follow the breeding plans made for me by the late Frances Mary Weaver of Sutherland Av fame. From her I learned that the backbone of a kennel is the quality of its females, always to keep the daughters of certain sires, always to line breed, to breed within the family and in that manner to hold fast to the best characteristics as they are gained. She told me, too how to outcross if and when a weakness crept in; to beware of light eyes, one of those faults extremely difficult to eradicate in future generations. Above all else, she advised strict adherence to type in preference to prettiness, and last but not least to remember without fail the old saying: "A coat can cover a multitude of sins."

My first good male, International Champion Sandee of Hesketh, was secured especially for mating to Ch. Grey Spider, to Natina of Hesketh and other lovely bitches of Hesketh breeding. Then came females of the Sutherland Av strain, and those great dogs suitable for them—Ch. Sutherland Av Tzueh, Int. Ch. Sutherland Av Hanshih and Tri-Int. Ch. Pierrot of Hartlebury, all Sutherland Av, all line-bred and going back to Sutherland Av Ouen-Teu-Tang.

From these pillars of the breed have descended more than 150 Orchard Hill champions, including such great winners as Ch. Jai Son Fu and his champion descendants which won from Coast to Coast. Space does not permit a listing of them here, many of them Pekingese Club Champions as well as Champions of Record. None will ever forget his beautiful daughter, Ch. Beh Tang, owned by Miss Dorothy Lathrop, which won not only Best in Show at the winter specialty, but repeated a great win at Westminster as best Pekingese and best toy dog in the show!

Mr. Royce won the specialty with a son, Ch. Jai Bee, and the Misses Lowther won it with a grandson, Ch. Silver Dust, while in California a great grandson, Ch. Piazzas Peppermint, won Best in

Madam Wellington Koo with Mr. Royce's Ch. Jai Bee on her lap, Miss Anna Katharine Nicholas standin

Show all breeds. Specialty show winners and other champions in Oregon and Washington State have Jai Son back in their pedigree.

The above record of achievement in the show ring I trust I may be pardoned for setting down. I do so not in praise of my own Jai Son, but solely to stress the point that *breeding counts*. This truth cannot be overemphasized. Pedigrees will disclose that some of the mentioned winners, not bred at Orchard Hill, resulted from outcrosses, but the dams were line-bred and good producers in themselves. With bitches of this caliber, a line-bred male descending from many generations of champions, as Jai Son was descended, is bound to produce progeny of correct type and show quality. We can make real progress only by careful pedigree study, by knowledge of the faults as well as the virtues of the individuals that comprise each pedigree, and by matings planned in such a way that heredity will perpetuate the good characters and wipe out or at least minimize the poor characters.

One of the beginner's first stumbling blocks lies in his choice of a stud. As a rule he wants to breed to the winning dog of the day. This is an easily understood yearning. We can forgive it and sympathize with the novice if, in the selection of the show-room's greatest winner as mate for his female, he applies the progeny test and finds it satisfactory. The beginner, of course, does not recognize the progeny test as such—he does not know what the words mean—but he applies it nevertheless. For, reduced to its simplest terms the progeny test means that the stud is a known producer of show-quality puppies. The novice sees outstanding youngsters sired by this stud he admires, so he believes he too can breed winners by using this dog for mating.

The fly in the ointment is this: The outstanding youngsters credited to the big winner, in practically every case owe their quality to the fact that the bloodlines of their dam coincide with the bloodlines of their sire. In other words, the breeding lay *within the family*. Now, if the pedigree of this novice's female disclosed the same family lines as the pedigree of the male, all well and good; if not, he would do better to purchase for the purpose a female possessed of the required breeding than he would to pay a stud fee for service to the best male on the circuit whose breeding was unsuitable.

Appearance is not everything; the properly planned mating must take into consideration pedigree as well. Seldom do we get show dogs from haphazard breeding, for the sire cannot shoulder entire responsibility for the litter. Both sire and dam contribute their share of characters to the offspring. In fact, a suitably line-bred bitch, though perhaps not of show quality herself, is apt to produce better puppies by the sire whose bloodlines coincide with hers than will the outcrossed bitch. Even in properly line-bred matings not all of the puppies will be of top show quality; at the same time, because all are bred within the family they may be regarded as potential producers of champions. Correctly bred themselves, they have a good chance of producing commendably but not otherwise except as lightning strikes.

The novice will make surer, quicker progress by investing in a line-bred matron, or in a line-bred puppy having good conformation, sturdy legs and dark eyes than he will in securing perhaps the flatter-faced show prospect that is *not* line-bred. The outcrossed female belongs to no particular strain, instead she is made up of a conglomeration of dissimilar inheritable characters descending possibly from several strains, and maybe each at war with the other because none have been intensified and fixed by *within the family* breeding. The outcrossed matron in rare instances has produced something as good as or better than herself, but one takes a long chance in expecting her to do so; whereas the correctly mated, outstanding line-bred matron is almost sure to hand down her commendable characteristics to her sons and daughters, or to later generations.

The line-bred matron of the quality under discussion is hard to find, harder to pay for. Suppose the novice cannot afford a line-bred show bitch! To some extent he can compromise by disregarding for the moment this thing called show quality and settle for a female of the plainer or less finished matron-type just so long as she has no glaring faults and is correctly line-bred. In fact, the line-bred female of matron-type will produce better stock in the long run than will the flatter-faced, more stylish show bitch lacking the proper genetic background.

When compelled for whatever reason to compromise on a line-bred matron-type female for breeding, we depend upon the intensification of the good characters in her pedigree to exert their influence in grading up the progeny. The female's appearance, we will say, is not all it might be, but her pedigree is! Therefore, we buttress that pedigree against another of the same kind for further reinforcement. Which means that as a mate for the female we select a stud from the same family—an uncle perhaps, a half brother, a grandfather or a cousin. At any rate, we choose the best possible male which in bloodlines coincides and which in appearance bids fair to correct the female's own shortcomings and hold the family type. Thus we restrict the number of different ancestors to a safe minimum and, if these ancestors are really good, the laws of heredity in all probability will see to it that the dam produces better specimens than herself.

The beginner cannot be expected to select the right stud for his female. Here again he must look to the experienced breeder for advice. Usually the stud owner with whom he confers has several dogs at service thus he may be well equipped to plan a suitable mating.

Suppose the stud fee is higher than the novice is willing to pay! He may be in a position to lay out the money yet be so new to the game that he does not realize the amount of initial costs. Later on he will learn what a substantial investment a top stud dog entails, but at the start he is usually floored with astonishment at the price asked for service. Never having owned a stud, he believes such fees are pure velvet hence oftentimes he cannot be persuaded to pay in advance for something that will not be delivered for nine weeks.

The larger share of stud services are paid for at the time of mating: there are occasions, however, where it is good business as well as admirable breeding technique for the stud owner to be lenient with the beginner in this respect. Particularly is this true where the stud owner knows that a higher-priced dog will be more suitable for the matron to be bred.

Customarily the novice takes his female for mating to the kennel from which he purchased it. Having made a friend of the breeder he has learned to depend upon the latter's advice. This is as it should be for the breeder knows his own stock and the manner in which it will probably reproduce.

In vogue are all sorts of compromise arrangements whereby the stud owner tries to save the beginner the shock of a sizeable stud fee. He may agree to accept one half of the fee at time of mating, the other half when the matron shows in whelp; he may breed for first choice of the litter, or for second choice, and so on. Such special arrangements, of course, are usually noted on the stud service receipt so that neither party to the contract will misunderstand or forget the exact terms.

Let us suppose now that the novice has followed the breeder's advice as to the selection of the right stud, and that the novice's first litter has arrived. The females from this litter if possible should be retained and the males sold. Then, by breeding these females back to a different male of the parent family, the novice begins to build his own strain. From this second litter he keeps the best male for later mating to his half sisters or grandmother, while the remaining male puppies he sells and uses the money for purchase of another matron. In this manner he defrays at least a portion of his expense at each step of his breeding program.

At this point it may be wise to consult with the larger kennel owners and from them learn what outcrosses have done well, exactly what such outcrosses have produced, then if these appear satisfactory to buy into that strain. Purchase of a proven matron is advisable, even an old one, for the purpose of securing complementary bloodlines. Of course, the year-old matron is the better buy, but these notes are written in the hope of assisting the modest beginner who may be unable to pay the prices warranted for young matrons or winners today.

Here are two examples of line-bred pedigrees:

Before leaving the question of line breeding, let me emphasize once more this fact: Line breeding *intensifies* the inheritable characters of the ancestors whatever they may be. It is the best method of perpetuating good characters. It is an equally sure method of perpetuating faults and weaknesses. The lesson is obvious. Therefore, the greatest care should be exercised in the selection of all breeding stock not only as regards intelligence and physical approach to the standard, but also as regards soundness, nerve steadiness and amenable disposition. Such faults as nervousness, shyness, viciousness and the like will be perpetuated to the same degree, unless of course they have been brought about by ignorant or careless handling.

PEDIGREE OF:
Ch. Jai Tao Wo of Orchard Hill
                                                Ch. Pier Jai Fu of Orchard Hill
                        Ch. Jai Fu's Son of Orchard Hill
                                                  H. Kho Jasmin of Orchard Hill
            Ch. Jai Son Fu of Orchard Hill
                                                  Vanity of Pechelee of Orchard Hill
                          Ch. Vans Panzee of Orchard Hill
                                                  Sudah of Orchard Hill
Jai Son's Atom of Orchard Hill
                                                 Tombo of Orchard Hill
                        Tombo's Tim of Pekestone
                                              Peppers Pole of Pekestone
            Tombo's Minty of Orchard Hill
                                              Pepper of Pekestone
                        Peppers Minty of Pekestone
                                            San Toy Katy

                                                Ch. Pier Jai Fu of Orchard Hill
                        Ch. Jai Fu's Son of Orchard Hill
                                          H. Kho Jasmin of Orchard Hill
            Ch. Jai Son Fu of Orchard Hill
                                               Vanity of Pechelee of Orchard Hill
                        Ch. Vans Panzee of Orchard Hill
                                              Sudah of Orchard Hill
Jai Son's Anora of Orchard Hill
                                               Ch. Jai Fu's Son of Orchard Hill
                        Ch. Jai Son Fu of Orchard Hill
                                             Ch. Vans Panzee of Orchard Hill
            Jai Son's Nora of Orchard Hill
                                               Ch. Remenham Wong of Orchard Hill
                        Wongs Anor of Orchard Hill
                                             Remenham Rosette

PEDIGREE OF:
Bon Jai Pixi of Orchard Hill
                                                Yu Sen Yu Chuo
                                Ch. Yu Sen Yu Toi of Orchard Hill
                                                Yu Sen Christina
                  Eng., Can., Am. & Cuban
                  Ch. Bonraye Fo Yu of Orchard Hill   Yu Sen Yu Chuo
                                Bonraye Chuo'ette
                                                Bonraye Memoree
Ch. Bonray Tony of Orchard Hill
                                               Ch. Jai Fu's Son of Orchard Hill
                                Ch. Jai Son Fu of Orchard Hill
                                             Ch. Vans Panzee of Orchard Hill
                  Cottage Hill Cindy
                                             Kai Choo Bee of Dahlyn
                                Malita of Dahlyn
                                             Bella of Wu San

                                             Ch. Jai Fu's Son of Orchard Hill
                                Ch. Jai Son Fu of Orchard Hill
                                             Ch. Vans Panzee of Orchard Hill
                  Ch. Jai Son Yat Sen of Orchard Hill
                                           Ch. Pier Simba of Orchard Hill
                                Ch. Simba Sara of Orchard Hill
                                             Pier Sudee of Orchard Hill
Ch. Jai Panzi of Orchard Hill
                                             Yu Sen Chuo Tu
                                Ch. Tulo of Alderbourne of Orchard Hill
                                             Charm of Elfann
                  Tulo's Jai Nie of Orchard Hill
                                             Pepper of Pekestone
                                Ch. Jai Nie of Orchard Hill
                                             Jai Panzee of Pekestone

Pedigrees showing line breeding.

6

Care of the Bred Bitch

THE first indispensable requisite for the breeding kennel of any size is a book of diary-like design to be used as a day book. I am not referring at the moment to the large, loose-leaf kennel record books obtainable commercially; these, with their separate sheets provided for pedigrees, stud and litter data, etc., are of course valuable and needed in the course of one's work. Instead, I mean the ordinary "day book" or kennel diary for quick reference.

In such a notebook is written all breeding dates, whelping dates and short daily happenings affecting each individual matron—her idiosyncrasies, her particular method of going about the business of whelping, her likes and dislikes perhaps, her reaction to various conditions. . . . Does she tire easily when walked or is she a little glutton for exercise. . . . Is she heedless in handling her unwieldy body or is she careful not to strike herself. . . . Does she ordinarily whelp early or late in her term, is she a fusser or is she one of those brave ones that always puts her best foot forward! Did we use pituitrin on this female last time, how did it affect her! Is she peculiarly sensitive to drugs? Such items as these, and many more, faithfully entered into the little book as they occur, will become an invaluable documentary regarding the reaction and performance of each kennel inmate. By the time the next litter is due, many of these details might be forgotten unless written down at the time. Hence the onset of each whelping finds memory refreshed and nursing facilities ready for the best possible care of the mother.

Whelping is but one phase of such record-keeping. It is equally valuable as regards stud services, diets, illness and convalescence. Purebred dogs as developed today are intelligent and individual. No two react alike. All have their funny notions, their strange obstinacies, their own special method of response to the ministrations of their masters. I believe the Pekingese is the most highly individual of all. To give these stout little hearts the care they deserve, one must understand them, and a prime source of understanding is the record written down.

Before attempting to describe the actual whelping suppose we consider first the question of prenatal care. Whether the matron be a world beater or also-ran, show specimen or pet, her success as a producer will very likely hinge upon her handling between mating time and parturition. Few save the most experienced among dog breeders realize the vital importance to puppy welfare of the type of existence provided for the matron while carrying her brood. Not alone the future health and ruggedness of every puppy, but the vigor and perhaps even the longevity of the mother herself may depend in some measure upon the care accorded her from the moment she is bred.

Absolute protection against the intrusion of male dogs is obligatory following the mating. As a rule the female will be more than ordinarily frisky and desirous of mating again, nor will she be at all particular about the selection of her consort; any dog will do. Consequently it becomes the order of the day to isolate her, as it were under lock and key, lest she mate again to some other male and jeopardize the breeder's best laid plans.

In this respect the well managed kennel scores over the home because the latter oftentimes does not have the facilities for safeguarding the bred bitch. The kennel dog can be shut up in her own compartment and allowed out only in her own exercising yard whereas the house dog has nothing but the eternal vigilance of her family to protect her.

Those breeding dogs in the home should keep this fact ever in mind, and see to it that for two weeks following the mating a locked room or other safe enclosure is guaranteed. Without number are instances wherein children have opened the door and let out the little mother-to-be, with disastrous results; and there are many cases of neglect among grown-ups to guard the female after breeding until she has returned to normal.

It is assumed that the female will have been checked by the veterinarian for worms prior to the breeding and of course inoculated against distemper; that she is in good flesh, well covered though not actually fat, and that she is vigorous and normal in all other respects.

For probably three weeks after mating she may be fed as usual, after which her special diet should be gradually introduced. Dietetic changes should be made slowly. Increase the proportion of liver and raw beef, decrease the proportion of starches and biscuit, at the same time stepping up the usual ration of cod liver oil. With an eagle eye watch the bowels. It is not unusual for constipation to set in and this, irrespective of any other complication, can be troublesome and difficult to treat because radical measures can never be resorted to while the female is carrying—no strong purgatives, no enemas, no drastic medication of any kind unless ordered by the attending veterinarian.

For constipation there is nothing better in my opinion than olive oil; not mineral oil, but a good grade of pure olive oil which has a mild loosening effect as well as a distinct food value. It also feeds the coat internally. One teaspoonful several times weekly or oftener if deemed necessary is enough. Under no circumstances give salts or castor oil.

When occasion seems to warrant, that is, when the condition refuses to respond to simpler measures, milk of magnesia may be used in small laxative doses. For really stubborn cases one teaspoon daily for a few days will suffice, or in milder cases one teaspoon several times a week. Laxative foods, too, should be given, namely, liver, orange juice, tomato juice and pieces of fruit, any or all of which have a distinctly beneficial effect. Pekes love small pieces of pared apple, pear, grapes, oranges, etc., also raw cabbage and lettuce.

In feeding the bred bitch try to think of her as the soil in which plants grow. Every flower, every apple, every bean takes something from the soil which must be returned to it if it is to retain its vitality. Otherwise, it will be too exhausted to produce another worthwhile crop. Each puppy is a fruit of the womb nourished from the resources of the mother's own body. Nature is more partial to the future than to the present wherefore she has no compunctions about robbing the dam for the sake of the young. If the matron is to retain her vigor for a reasonable period of years she must be nourished in quantity and quality sufficient for herself as well as for her litter. And the nutrients must be of protein or building type to greater extent than of carbohydrate or energy type.

From the moment the female begins to show in whelp, when she rounds out and looks definitely heavier she must be handled with all possible caution. In lifting her use both hands. Spread the palm of the left hand between her front legs with her chest resting on the palm, then shove the right palm between the hind legs so that the little stomach may rest comfortably on palm and forearm. This lift which provides perfect support without strain anywhere should always be employed when transferring a bitch to the grooming table or when lifting her for any other purpose such as carrying upstairs or outdoors for exercise.

With her naturally short legs and underslung build, the Peke in whelp runs a thousand risks of striking her underbody if permitted to jump or in any manner exert herself to reach varied levels. She must not be allowed to jump up on the sofa or on chairs of any sort, to go up or down stairs or to negotiate a height of one single step. The house dog had best be kept on the ground floor and led out on leash for exercise; carried across street intersections to avoid any attempt to leap over the curb. In short, she should be walked only on level ground uncluttered by obstructions. Remember, the smallest step up may strike or cause dangerous strain.

Exercise for the bred bitch is highly necessary and will without doubt contribute to the general health as well as to vigorous parturition. Strength of the entire hind-leg structure has bearing upon normal whelping and such strength, I believe, is best developed by the measured peg-peg of leash walking.

While Pekingese are sufficiently rugged to go abroad in any weather, there are two things especially to be guarded against, namely, slippery surfaces and excessive heat. Icy sidewalks and even pavements made slippery by recent showers may risk a fall which, however slight, can prove disastrous to dam and future litter. Excessive heat also the Pekingese cannot stand when well along in whelp, so exercise in the heat of a summer's day is taboo. Preferably, select a shady place away from traffic and strange-dog annoyance or, better, walk only in the evening when the weather is extremely warm. In moderate temperatures, however, the bred bitch should have two or three regular exercise periods daily, several short walks being more beneficial than one long one. Exercise but do not overtire; stimulate but do not exhaust. And always wait at least one half-hour after feeding before starting out.

In attempting to gauge the exercise distance best suited to the average female, remember that distance is no proper criterion, the length of stride being the unalterable common denominator of mileage. The small dog takes innumerable steps to get places; he has to, especially when his legs are short, and the effort entailed in each one of those steps requires the expenditure of the same amount of energy as does the longer stride of the larger dog. So judge distance on that basis and avoid too hurried a pace.

The average Pekingese in whelp should be walked no more than a quarter of a mile at a time without rest. When she becomes very heavy her walks may well be shorter, more frequent and slow-motion. The drag of the carried litter seems more pronounced in some females than in others, irrespective of the vigor and previous exercising habits of the individual. This the owner must watch carefully as he guides his charge along. If the female pants unduly and sits down often to rest, do not attempt to force her to walk farther for the moment. Sit down by the roadside with her, or pick her up and carry her a little way, and then proceed as before.

The novice breeder as well as the pet owner with his first female is sometimes astonished at mention of the fact that the pregnant bitch must be protected against falls. I suppose they consider the quadruped firmly enough planted on four feet to obviate the possibility of coming to harm through loss of balance! Much of the time, however, the modern dog walks on surfaces too hard and unyielding to permit adequate purchase by the claws hence is just as subject to slipping and falling as is the human being.

What the dog gains by means of his all-four posture he loses through the artificial medium for his stance. And when he does lose his balance he can rarely right himself before he goes down because, being a quadruped, he cannot wave or rotate his forelegs to re-establish balance as can man. A female does not have to fall far in order to injure or perhaps kill one puppy: a dead puppy may possibly infect the lot and certainly is more difficult to expel.

Protecting the bred bitch against falls in the home can be quite a problem especially where the pet has enjoyed the run of the house. Here we have stairs and chairs, sofas and ottomans, front doors and back doors and like assorted obstructions and escapes through which the female may come to harm. It is therefore essential that some safe cache be arranged. An ordinary baby pen is excellent, or a knock-down wire pen can be constructed at small expense and set up in a quiet room during those few critical weeks. A roomy closet, if sufficiently well ventilated can be utilized, with an extendable wire window screen spread across the doorway. Of course, the larger such enclosures are the better; even so, a fairly small one is to be preferred to a fall.

Psychological handling is as vital to safety as manual handling. Keep the mother-to-be happy and contented. Rough-housing with her kennel companions which hitherto may have constituted one of her especial pleasures is now definitely out as a form of exercise or amusement. It is not unusual for kennel dogs to strike up great friendships among their own kind and they miss such associations keenly when set apart while in whelp. If time forbids the owner to give these lonely ones much individual attention, the lack can be made up by selecting as companion a dependable, staid and well-mannered older dog not addicted to rough play.

But one must be very sure that no fights occur, nor even short-lived little scuffles which, no matter how superficial in their argumentativeness, might harm the matron physically or worry her emotionally. Also, country life suggests absolute ban on chasing squirrels and chipmunks, or streaking after cats just for the fun of it. When opportunity offers, Pekingese do all of these things with as great an abandon as do larger dogs.

However, one cannot with impunity cut out all pleasurable pursuits merely because a female has been bred. The trick is to substitute something else of less hazardous proportions, namely, little interludes each day of personal companionship with the owner or with someone in whom the matron has confidence. Fondling, soft-talk, approbation all have their place in making the female happy and instilling the feeling of security to maintain nervous equilibrium which is one common denominator of physical health.

Cats make perfect foster mothers.

The Quigley Whelping Box.

As soon as the bitch is thought to be in whelp, provide a suitable box or basket. We use a wicker basket with high, rounded back and 6-inch front. I prefer the high back because in cold weather a woolen blanket or shawl can be draped over sides and top to protect the puppies from draft. In the basket we place several thicknesses of newspapers which give the prospective mother something to scratch up and make a proper bed for her young.

The Quigley Box for mother and puppies can also be used at whelping time, instead of the high-backed basket. These boxes have two fronts. The six inch front is used for the first month; then as the puppies get older and try to crawl over the front, the 8-inch one is put in place. Grooves at the sides hold these removable fronts; the dam can get in and out, but the puppies cannot get over the higher front. Later, the front is removed and the puppies go out into their pen, using the box as their bedroom. Note the half-rounds fastened to the three sides. They are thick enough to keep the dam from accidentally crushing a puppy as it makes a space where a puppy can get between her back and the box sides. There is also a hinged top, half of which can be laid back or kept down depending on room temperature. There is also a 2-inch space at the back under the slightly raised floor, where a heating pad, set at low heat, is placed under the box floor. These boxes are 18″ x 18″ x 18″ and are light weight plywood.

Made ready well in advance of the whelping the female learns to regard the basket or box as her own special retreat, and to it she will repair as a matter of course when she begins to feel definitely uncomfortable. Its preparation delayed too close to the due date, the whelping bed may prove too strange to be entirely acceptable.

WHELPING CALENDAR

Find the month and date on which your bitch was bred in one of the left-hand columns. Directly opposite that date, in the right-hand column, is her expected date of whelping, bearing in mind that 61 days is as common as 63.

Date bred January	Date due to whelp March	Date bred February	Date due to whelp April	Date bred March	Date due to whelp May	Date bred April	Date due to whelp June	Date bred May	Date due to whelp July	Date bred June	Date due to whelp August	Date bred July	Date due to whelp September	Date bred August	Date due to whelp October	Date bred September	Date due to whelp November	Date bred October	Date due to whelp December	Date bred November	Date due to whelp January	Date bred December	Date due to whelp February
1	5	1	5	1	3	1	3	1	3	1	3	1	2	1	3	1	3	1	3	1	3	1	2
2	6	2	6	2	4	2	4	2	4	2	4	2	3	2	4	2	4	2	4	2	4	2	3
3	7	3	7	3	5	3	5	3	5	3	5	3	4	3	5	3	5	3	5	3	5	3	4
4	8	4	8	4	6	4	6	4	6	4	6	4	5	4	6	4	6	4	6	4	6	4	5
5	9	5	9	5	7	5	7	5	7	5	7	5	6	5	7	5	7	5	7	5	7	5	6
6	10	6	10	6	8	6	8	6	8	6	8	6	7	6	8	6	8	6	8	6	8	6	7
7	11	7	11	7	9	7	9	7	9	7	9	7	8	7	9	7	9	7	9	7	9	7	8
8	12	8	12	8	10	8	10	8	10	8	10	8	9	8	10	8	10	8	10	8	10	8	9
9	13	9	13	9	11	9	11	9	11	9	11	9	10	9	11	9	11	9	11	9	11	9	10
10	14	10	14	10	12	10	12	10	12	10	12	10	11	10	12	10	12	10	12	10	12	10	11
11	15	11	15	11	13	11	13	11	13	11	13	11	12	11	13	11	13	11	13	11	13	11	12
12	16	12	16	12	14	12	14	12	14	12	14	12	13	12	14	12	14	12	14	12	14	12	13
13	17	13	17	13	15	13	15	13	15	13	15	13	14	13	15	13	15	13	15	13	15	13	14
14	18	14	18	14	16	14	16	14	16	14	16	14	15	14	16	14	16	14	16	14	16	14	15
15	19	15	19	15	17	15	17	15	17	15	17	15	16	15	17	15	17	15	17	15	17	15	16
16	20	16	20	16	18	16	18	16	18	16	18	16	17	16	18	16	18	16	18	16	18	16	17
17	21	17	21	17	19	17	19	17	19	17	19	17	18	17	19	17	19	17	19	17	19	17	18
18	22	18	22	18	20	18	20	18	20	18	20	18	19	18	20	18	20	18	20	18	20	18	19
19	23	19	23	19	21	19	21	19	21	19	21	19	20	19	21	19	21	19	21	19	21	19	20
20	24	20	24	20	22	20	22	20	22	20	22	20	21	20	22	20	22	20	22	20	22	20	21
21	25	21	25	21	23	21	23	21	23	21	23	21	22	21	23	21	23	21	23	21	23	21	22
22	26	22	26	22	24	22	24	22	24	22	24	22	23	22	24	22	24	22	24	22	24	22	23
23	27	23	27	23	25	23	25	23	25	23	24	23	24	23	25	23	25	23	25	23	25	23	24
24	28	24	28	24	26	24	26	24	26	24	26	24	25	24	26	24	26	24	26	24	26	24	25
25	29	25	29	25	27	25	27	25	27	25	27	25	26	25	27	25	27	25	27	25	27	25	26
26	30	26	30	26	28	26	28	26	28	26	28	26	27	26	28	26	28	26	28	26	28	26	27
27	31	27	May 1	27	29	27	29	27	29	27	29	27	28	27	29	27	29	27	29	27	29	27	28
28	Apr. 1	28	2	28	30	28	30	28	30	28	30	28	29	28	30	28	30	28	30	28	30	28	Mar. 1
29	2			29	31	29	July 1	29	31	29	31	29	30	29	31	29	30	29	31	29	31	29	2
30	3			30	June 1	30	2	30	Aug. 1	30	Sep. 1	30	Oct. 1	30	Nov. 1	30	2	30	Jan. 1	30	Feb. 1	30	3
31	4			31	2			31	2			31	2	31	2			31	2			31	4

Reproduction by courtesy of the Gaines Dog Research Center, N.Y.C.

106

7
Whelping

WHATEVER the degree of his experience, the kennel owner will require the services of the veterinarian from time to time, yet I believe there is such a thing as too great reliance upon professional assistance in the care of one's dogs.

Some breeders throw up their hands at the slightest sign of indisposition in puppies or grown dogs while others expect the veterinarian to be present at every whelping. The up-to-date, small animal practitioner is an extremely busy man not always immediately available for each emergency. Therefore, the breeder will do well to learn as early as possible in his doggy career to shoulder the responsibilities of his charges' minor ailments; and certainly he should know enough about the intricacies of parturition to see his matrons safely through their normal whelping. I believe also that the breeder who learns to supervise the whelping of his own females derives infinitely greater satisfaction from his hobby.

Pekingese whelp from the fifty-eighth to the sixty-fourth day following the mating. Observe the female carefully right along. By the fourth or fifth week she will begin to take on flesh; she looks as if she were too fat all over. Gradually the size of the abdomen increases, the underslung appearance of the body being more pronounced as the carried litter sags. Toward the end of the term, the backbone becomes gaunt. This can be felt with the fingers even if it cannot be noted beneath the coat.

Normally the female will evidence signs of distress several days in advance of parturition. She may refuse to eat and certainly she will exhibit a new type of restlessness, a sort of perpetual hunt and poke into all manner of places. She will scratch up and dig into her sleeping basket as if she were preparing a bundle of wash for the laundry. This is a first rate sign that the puppies will shortly be born.

Of course, exceptions to the usual order of fussing abound, wherein females of ultra modern stamp sit around apathetically with a "let George do it" attitude. These are not invariably the difficult whelpers either; they have been known to deliver their puppies by rapid transit route, that is, after a minimum of pacing and panting. Even so, the normal behavior consists of vigorous bed-making coupled with an air of real distress.

At this time an extra good grooming is indicated. With blunt, rounded scissors cut away the hair from around the nipples. If the skirts are unusually long and thick, trim off much of this hair also, especially around the vulva. The matron will lose her coat anyway after her puppies are weaned so it is no sacrifice to take the hair from the underbody and beneath the tail. In fact, grooming of the sort contributes to the ease and cleanliness of delivery, and the puppies find the nipples more readily than when hidden in the mother's coat.

After removing as much of the hair as seems necessary, thoroughly clean the nipples and stomach with cotton and alcohol, taking care to clean off any dark secretions from the nipples where worm eggs may cluster and risk being swallowed by the babies as they nurse.

Watch the patient closely for the first sign of labor pains which will be noted as straining regularly timed and increasing in force, sometimes as long as two hours before a puppy is expelled. Theoretically, nature furnishes a series of pains sufficient for the expulsion of each puppy; usually the birth of the first takes longer, the remainder following more rapidly when the whelping proceeds normally. From the instant the first strain is noted, the matron ought not to be left alone.

Some females whelp more easily than others, but until one has observed the whelping of many litters he may not know when the crucial moment arrives. Ordinarily it is as the sudden hush following the storm; rampaging ceases, restlessness is gone. The matron sits down, gathers her forces for the final tussle. You can almost see her grit her teeth as she gives a powerful stretch with her entire body, then settles down to a herculean strain. The parts above the vulva swell noticeably as the foetus rounds the pelvic girdle, descends and finally starts to emerge like a shiny, black bubble. Each strain brings the puppy farther down and out; if the birth is normal the entire fluid-filled sac containing the puppy is expelled.

Especially in the case of a first litter is the young matron apt to grow frightened, so panicky oftentimes that she will do nothing to release the puppy from its enclosing sac and sever the umbilical cord. When outside the body, the sac must be opened without delay, so when the dam does not recognize the emergency instinctively, as she probably will not, the attendant breaks open the membrane around the head with the fingers thus releasing the puppy and enabling it to breathe immediately.

Clean squares of toweling or muslin should be at hand to wipe the baby's head and mouth at once else fluid may get into the lungs and cause pneumonia. This is the answer to those mysterious puppy deaths during the first few days.

With the puppy free of the sac and its head dried, we now gather the sac and cord together, holding them with one of the muslin squares. With small artery forceps hold the cord to forestall any slipping back, and with very gentle traction, endeavor to loosen and bring away the afterbirth which is attached to the cord.

The idea of the artery forceps clamped to the cord is to prevent strain on the cord during even this gentle traction which might result in umbilical hernia. The traction is exerted on the afterbirth which is still in or partially in the body. Hold fast to the clamp and, if the afterbirth does not come at once, keeping trying to remove it at intervals. Do not actually pull as the afterbirth may shred and break; use merely very gentle traction timed exactly as the matron strains. It is a serious matter when the cord breaks and the afterbirth is retained so *gentle* pulling is imperative.

Artery forceps have replaced the old fashioned method of hand-tying the cord. Have several on hand—a second puppy may arrive before the first afterbirth is released, and so another will be needed for the next puppy. If the afterbirth does not come away at once, cut the umbilical cord between the clamp and the puppy's stomach leaving if possible an inch-long stump to prevent rupture. Serious bleeding can result from cutting too close to the body, hence, the longer stump is advisable. An added precaution against infection, in cases where the stump is too short, is to apply a very small amount of metaphen.

Except in rare cases each puppy has its own sac and its own afterbirth, the two being connected by the cord. Each afterbirth must be secured and brought away else septicemia and dreaded metritis may follow with loss of the mother in most instances, to say nothing of the necessity for hand-feeding the orphans or raising them on a foster mother. Watch the matron every moment; an afterbirth may be expelled when least expected and be devoured by the dam. If there has been no chance of this, and if an afterbirth is still unaccounted for, administer a dose of castor oil—one teaspoonful for the female of average size.

The owner should have learned how to handle a hypodermic syringe. If he does not, then he should call in the veterinarian who will inject one half c.c. of pituitrin in the upper leg muscle; this, of course, after the whelping has been completed. Pituitrin stimulates the labor pains, hence, further straining resulting from the pituitrin often brings the missing afterbirth. It is used also to stimulate uterine action when labor pains are not sufficiently strong to bring the second puppy.

After each puppy is born and the cord is cut, dry the little one thoroughly and put it to the breast. With the mother leave one or two strong puppies to nurse and to stimulate uterine contractions. Place the others in a small box lined with a blanket that has been warmed by the low heat of an electric heating pad. The latter, which must have a waterproof covering, is placed in the box first, the blanket over it.

Each time the bitch gives birth to a puppy keep drying her off, keep dry newspapers under her, and when she is finished give her an extra good drying. If her skirts have been trimmed, any washing of her hindparts will be unnecessary until the following day. Keep a thick padding of newspapers in the basket and a single blanket over the papers. When all the puppies have arrived and are safely nursing encourage the mother to clean them, especially to lick beneath their little tails.

Throughout the normal whelping or shortly thereafter, the dam should be allowed all the lukewarm milk she will drink. Though she rarely cries she does pant a great deal, hence loses considerable fluid which has to be made up to her in the form of drinking. We all know that the nursing mother needs milk for the sake of its incomparable nutrients; actually, I find a great many matrons refuse to take it the first few days except immediately after whelping. Those first drinks of milk are often all the food she will touch until after the third day. We humor the new mother by holding right up to her a saucer of whole, rich milk; we even hold it in the basket if need be. Perhaps she drinks it solely because of this special attention, whereas she would not deign to touch it at any other time. And should she be exhausted by a long, hard whelping, give her ten drops of good brandy in a teaspoonful of milk, repeating several times if weakness or general apathy is still noted.

Now for the real examination of the puppies! Make sure there are no cleft palates. Detection of the cleft palate is sometimes difficult as it may be slight and located far back in the mouth. Open each mouth gently. If a deeply indented slit or cleft in the roof of the mouth is noted, put the unfortunate baby to sleep without delay. He hasn't a chance; he will only starve to death. The incomplete joining of the mouth-roof bone leaves an opening into the nasal cavity which permits the milk to flow out through the nose, or if the milk does manage to go down it is apt to get into the lungs and cause death by traumatic pneumonia. I have tried to raise these cleft palate cases by hand feeding but they always die so it is merciful to chloroform them immediately. Indeed it is a great temptation to try to save them for invariably they seem to be the best in the litter, but years of experience have taught me it is only a heartbreaking waste of time.

Not infrequently cleft palates are accompanied by hind-leg deformities wherein the hind legs turn in and sometimes back toward the abdomen; they do not stretch out behind in natural position for traction as the puppy attempts to nurse. Such malformation is often apparent when the opening or crack in the roof of the mouth is pronounced. However, hind leg deformity may be present without any imperfection in the mouth, that is, the roof of the mouth may be completely closed over and still the hind legs turn in. Therefore, do not destroy the puppy whose hind legs appear deformed unless the mouth is definitely cleft. The cleft palate is hopeless; the turned-in hind legs, in themselves, are not.

Hind legs may be slightly turned-in at birth as a result of pressure while the litter is carried. For instance, the puppies of the small female with the large litter may suffer malforming pressure; also in a litter of moderate number one over-large puppy may press upon the foetus lying next to it. If turned-in hind legs are caused by neither mineral deficiency nor utilization, that is, if they have been brought about by pressure alone, they can probably be massaged back to normal. Work on them three or four times per week, gently rubbing the legs bones between thumb and forefinger to stimulate circulation. Then when a little strength in the legs is noted, as the baby tries to push himself along, ever so carefully turn the feet out so he can exert force in the natural position.

The preceding paragraphs have dealt with normal delivery when all goes as nature intended. However, difficult whelping is not exceptional when an expert veterinarian, the specialist in small animal practice, must be called in. At the same time there are certain types of abnormalities with which the breeder has learned to cope fairly well. One of these is what is termed breech presentation. In a normal delivery the head emerges first while in breech presentation the hindparts come first. As it is not unusual I am going to give a few tips on this type of delivery which may be of assistance to beginners.

When the puppy is large and the straining violent and prolonged, the sac often ruptures inside the body. The hind legs protrude and the puppy is wedged, its head caught in the pelvic girdle. Needless to say, it must be released before the puppy smothers, for the moment the sac is opened the little one must have air.

If the puppy is caught in this manner, its hips and hind legs hanging, an assistant holds the matron in standing position on a table. With a square of muslin or a washcloth in the hand, grasp around the puppy's hips and gently pull down. In thus attempting to dislodge the puppy, exert the pull downward as if trying to bring it between the matron's legs and up toward her stomach. This directional pulling often releases the head, which is caught by its chin, and brings it out without injury. If the mistake is made of pulling the puppy straight out when it is caught in the pelvic girdle, the neck may be broken. Released in time, and the neck uninjured, the puppy can be made to breathe by hard rubbing and by artificial respiration. It will help, too, to swing the baby up and down, holding the mouth open with tongue depressed—use one finger for this. The swinging motion may start the breathing by forcing air into the lungs. A small bottle of aromatic spirits of ammonia, opened and held to the mouth, is another way to induce breathing. However, do not touch the tongue with the undiluted ammonia as it will burn the membranes. Those who understand mouth to mouth resuscitation can induce breathing and save many of these puppies.

The puppy stuck at the shoulders may be delivered safely by the following method. Scrub and disinfect the hands thoroughly, cut closely the nail of the forefinger or put on a sterile rubber fingerstall. Squeeze some KY jelly into the vagina and around the caught puppy. Also lubricate well the index finger which is then inserted each side of the front shoulders and forelegs hooked down, then pull the puppy out as before described.

If the puppy is presented hind feet first, with the stomach *up,* then the little body must be turned around so that the hind legs, hips and stomach are *down,* before any effort is made to complete the delivery. Just as in the case described in the preceding paragraph, the head is caught but in that position it cannot be released without injury. Using lots of jelly as a lubricant, insert the forefinger and turn the body so that hips and stomach are down, then grasp the hips, pulling down and under.

Keep in mind above all that whelping requires a tremendous expenditure of strength by the dam, that she can exhaust herself with the effort before even one puppy is born. Six hours of straining, sometimes less, is about all a female can stand. Unsuccessful in delivering a puppy within that time, she should be examined by a competent veterinarian who can determine whether or not a Caesarean is needed. Usually the birth of one puppy opens the way for the remainder of the litter without hindrance; occasionally, however, trouble is encountered after the first due to faulty presentation, to an overlarge foetus, to uterine exhaustion when no further labor pains are observed, or to the general exhaustion of the dam herself. At any rate, if the first puppy is not born within five or six hours after straining starts, or if more than two hours elapses between deliveries, it is advisable to consult the veterinarian at once.

Caesareans are not unusual among purebred dogs; in many cases they are highly successful provided the female is vigorous and not over-tired by suffering and delay. Few bitches can survive such an operation if a puppy has previously been taken with instruments, or if the mother has been allowed to strain too long. If a Caesarean is needed it should be done promptly, before exhaustion sets in or before possible infection from the use of instruments.

We have had very good luck with Caesareans in cases where the operation has been performed in time. Ordinarily we administer one half c.c. of pituitrin if the uterus is open and well dilated. We then wait a reasonable time, at least six hours, before resorting to the operation. There is such a thing as rushing in to operate too quickly. Give nature every chance to do her work; if it is evident that she cannot under existing conditions then by all means get a skilled surgeon to operate before the matron wears herself out.

Penicillin and the sulfa drugs have nullified much of the former risk of Caesareans, and if the surgeon is competent and the bitch not exhausted or already infected, the outcome is favorable. The puppies nurse without seeming to hurt the mother in the process, and the wound soon heals. As to the site of the incision, we prefer the medial line. We find it easier for the bitch as she can lie comfortably on either side and the medial line on the belly has less hair and is easier to keep clean. The foregoing information, of course, I give merely as personal experience: the details of the operation and subsequent treatment are for the surgeon in charge to decide. Here I must add Pekingese are often allergic to morphine and to chloroform, but before using the latter a shot of atropin, will help dry up saliva and prevent gagging and choking while the anesthetic is being given.

How many puppies are we to expect? This is the burning question of the inexperienced who, it would seem, are inclined to count their chickens before they are hatched! The breeder whose matron has produced four puppies, safe and sound, has every right to that glow of satisfaction which follows things accomplished. This is the number of the larger share of Pekingese litters, in fact, it is quite enough for a dog so small to whelp and raise. If you get two or three you may still count yourself fortunate for, as has been said again and again, good things seldom come in large packages. Oftentimes, litters consist of five or six, the record number for the breed of eight having been whelped at the O'Palart Kennels of the late Mrs. Bertha Hanson.

As a rule a matron has three well developed nipples on each side, occasionally four, but few females can supply enough milk for more than five or six puppies at best. When we have large litters here we give one or two of the babies to a bitch that has whelped at about the same time. When we have three or perhaps four matrons whelping a few days apart, we divide the puppies evenly between them, by a method of transfer described in detail in the next following chapter.

Famous Alderbournes, owned by the Misses Ashton Cross, include Ch. Yu Tong of Alderbourne, sire of Ch. Tong Tuo.

Ch. Tong Tuo, sire of Ch. Lin Yu Tang and lovely Tulyar.

8

The Matron and Her Nestlings

ORDINARILY when the whelping is completed the bitch seems relaxed, tired but happy. Especially if she is an old hand, she takes great satisfaction in tending her brood and though constantly alert to their needs she appears at ease. The novice breeder, too, is relieved that the ordeal is over, but he must be certain that *it is over*. Cases are on record where a delayed puppy has been whelped twenty-four hours after all had apparently been delivered.

Watch the matron closely. Any stiffness or hunching of the back should be regarded with suspicion while a hard lump resembling a head, felt in the abdomen by gentle palpation with the fingers, may indicate one more puppy to come. Too, panting, tenseness or greenish discharge accompanied by a rise in temperature call for veterinary examination.

When all the puppies have arrived, are well dried off and comfortably nursing, the electric pad on low heat can be placed on the floor *under* the basket (except in extremely hot weather), and left there for twenty-four hours or until the bitch gives evidence of being a good mother desirous of staying in with her puppies. The little ones must not become chilled; this the accomplished mother knows instinctively as she huddles herself around them trying to warm them with her own body heat. Once in a while young or highly nervous females do not get down to the business of mothering for the first few days. They may be frightened with the ordeal, or so jittery that they have no notion of how to nest the babies together against their breasts. Be patient with these, allowing time for the real firing of the maternal instinct.

The new-born puppies of course are lying on a blanket while another blanket is close by to cover the little ones when the dam is put out to exercise in the kennel runway. Even if she is disinclined to leave her family, as many are for the first two weeks, she should be sent or taken out four times daily at least, and if the weather is unfavorable she must be carefully dried before going back to her basket or box.

A satisfactory arrangement for mother and litter is a pen or separate enclosure, floored with newspapers, where the basketful of babies can be unmolested. Fresh water should be constantly available, and a saucer of milk may well be provided twice each day if the matron will take it. Here she can enjoy a certain amount of freedom. She can nurse her brood as required, but she can hop out of the box and get away from them at intervals if she wishes. This modicum of exercise is beneficial. If she spends a reasonable amount of time with the puppies, if they feel plump and firm to the hand signifying adequate nourishment, and if the weather is not freezing, then the electric pad may be removed. Each morning after the mother has exercised, groom her thoroughly and clean off any dried secretions or dirt that might be swallowed by the puppies, brushing and combing out all loose hair and note condition of the nipples.

The house-pet mother, which ordinarily lacks regular kennel facilities, should be given a room of her own where she can be by herself in peace and quiet and without too much strong light. This is particularly important in the case of the young bitch, as during the earlier nursing period she may be nervously upset and try to remove her babies from the basket and hide them. We are too hasty oftentimes to brand such a female a poor mother, when all she requires is peace and quiet and gentle handling. Given all three, even the flightiest soon settle down and make good mothers.

In the rearing of puppies scrupulous cleanliness is obligatory. The blanket on which the little ones lie must be turned, brushed and changed when soiled, several times daily if need be and certainly once each twenty-four hours. All cleaning up of the bed should be done while the matron is outside, for many bitches resent the handling of their young. Though usually docile and friendly, they have been known to grow quite fierce, maybe to snap and bite. Gentleness and quiet, soothing address is the understanding owner's answer to such apparently strange conduct on the part of the mother whose disposition in reality has not changed but whose solicitude for her babies makes her fear for their welfare.

The owner himself or herself once in a while is unwittingly responsible for the suddenly aggressive attitude of the dam. Pleased beyond measure with the nestful of babies, the owner admires them without stint, perhaps forgetting that the matron has lately come through a severe ordeal and would appreciate a little admiration for herself as a needed pickup. Dogs are highly sensitive to praise and the lack of it; when they have every right to expect it and do not get it, they may grow temporarily surly from jealousy and disappointment.

This psychological problem is difficult for the new breeder to understand. He thinks the maternal instinct is everything, that it governs the dam's every thought and act. It probably does with most domesticated animals, but the dog's allegiance is divided between her young and her master—even the primal urge to protect her young is underwritten by her love for man and her desire to serve him as well. These puppies are the greatest gift she can offer. Thank her, then by patting her gently and telling her, before the babies are even touched, what an admirable little soul she is.

With the matron outside and the bed straightened up, take stock of the puppies. Individual handling enables one to gauge the progress of each, to detect which are plump and comparatively heavy in the hand and which are small and slightly thin. Any that appear frail should be held to the best nipples, that is, to those which are easiest to pull. Customarily the front or upper nipples are harder to grasp and hold, and they require stronger suction to promote the flow; while the lower or rear breasts which usually are better filled require but a tiny tug to bring the milk down. With amazing rapidity even very young puppies learn which are the best seats at the table, and so we find the huskiest tots making tracks for the more delicious nipples where they hang on like leeches, leaving the frailer babes to take pot luck.

Supervision of the nursing for the first few days will promote at least a certain amount of uniformity in puppy strength. Without such supervision the less vigorous puppies will fall off rapidly; they will be shunted to the side of the basket because the dam by nature does not favor weaklings. But if the owner sees to it that all get equal chance at the breasts, the frail ones soon fill out and gain enough strength to fight for themselves.

See that all in the litter nurse at the same time, at least every three hours, otherwise the greedy ones will milk the breasts dry for the time being and nothing will be left for the others. Especially in the case of large litters it may be advisable to keep the bitch away from the basket for a short period until nursing time—this gives the breasts an opportunity to fill. Or, if more convenient, separate the strong puppies from the weak. Place the strong ones in an adjoining box equipped of course with blanket and pad, and put these to the matron after the weaker tykes have nursed. This entails additional work though not as much work as it is to resort to artificial feeding with the necessary sterilization of bottles, nipples or droppers and like paraphernalia which is quite a chore in itself.

Fortunate is the breeder who has several litters whelped a few days apart, when the weak ones from each batch can be segregated and given to the best mother, and the larger ones of equal size apportioned to another. Few matrons resent such interchange of puppies if properly done, in fact, I have had only a few that knew the difference.

When re-apportioning puppies to different dams, put the mothers outside for half an hour. Puppies that are to be transferred should be placed *under* the new dam's own puppies and under her blanket so that all will smell alike. Leave them beneath the blanket, then when the mother is brought in and placed with them, squeeze a little of her milk on the adopted babies and hold them to her back nipples, at the same time holding her own babies to her front nipples.

In case the mother notices the strangers, keep her licking them if possible; and when all have had their fill, put her out again for another hour or so, covering the puppies as before. Watch the mother carefully when she returns to the basket to learn whether she accepts them all. Occasionally it becomes necessary to put the dam outside three or four times before complete acceptance of the strangers but to date we have never had a mother refuse stranger-puppies when this procedure is followed. The sole exception to the rule is where a puppy has gone off so badly that it is too weak to nurse, or when perchance it may have nursed acid milk and is so poisoned it emits a bad odor—this baby the mother will push aside exactly as its own mother would do.

If the litter is not doing well and the puppies emit a reedy squeak, we suspect acid milk and immediately place on the tongue of each a pinch of bisurated magnesia powder. If pain is present and stomach distended give a salt-spoon of warm olive oil to which has been added two drops of brandy. The magnesia powder can be given twice daily, while the mother should have a teaspoonful of milk of magnesia every morning for at least five days. Also, add a pinch of bicarbonate of soda to her food, or, if she is not eating well, add one-half teaspoon of soda to her drinking water, allowing two cups of water to the drinking vessel. The soda can do no harm. If the bitch has not raised a previous litter it is advisable to start the soda in her drinking water three days or more before she is due to whelp.

The dam takes entire charge of the puppies' toilet. Ostensibly, her periodic licking is designed to keep the babies clean, actually the ministrations of her tongue serve a more deep-seated purpose. By its massage it increases the circulation and aids in keeping the body warm; by its efficient washing of eyes, nose and mouth, it forestalls incrustations from slobbered milk which might irritate the membranes and even cause infection; and by wiping off the hindparts with characteristic rotary motion, it stimulates bowel movement and prevents caking. This last service is the most important.

Occasionally the mother does not keep all puppies clean under the tail—it is no easy job when the litter is large, and sometimes females just do not take kindly to this phase of care. Hindparts must then be hand-cleaned several times daily with cotton and vaseline. The fastidious mother can often be encouraged to keep the puppy's undertail clean if it is first daubed with some foreign substance like vaseline. Then hand the puppy, hind-end to her, when usually she will lick if off with a "I don't want to, but I suppose I must" attitude.

The mother's breasts will require constant watching with practiced eye. It is a well known fact that puppies prefer certain nipples and tend to leave others alone. Each breast is a separate little milk container with its outlet, the nipple; hence, if one breast is not nursed regularly and thus relieved of the pressure of its load, it may become swollen, hard and caked.

The caked breast, if noted early, can be alleviated by very tender finger-milking, and warm vinegar applied. If neglected and the milk cannot be drawn off, apply warm camphorated oil several times daily. Do this after the puppies have nursed, and keep the dam away for several hours. Then with alcohol clean the oil from the affected breast before the puppies are permitted to nurse. Unless the caked breast is caught in time and relieved by means of the vinegar or camphorated oil treatment as outlined, an abscess may form and break down. The abscess must be lanced and penicillin administered by the veterinarian.

After whelping, the bitch's diet should be regulated on a basis of each individual case. If there is no danger of infection present, and all afterbirths have come, the regular diet will be in order. Meat, fat and biscuit may be continued, with the addition of all the milk or milk foods the dam will take. If she likes milk, it can be made very nourishing with raw egg beaten into it. One egg in a cup of whole milk, half a cup given in the morning, the balance in the evening, will provide the needed calcium, protein and fat so vital at this time because the large litter depletes the mother's system particularly of its calcium supply. A teaspoonful of lime water may be added to the cup of milk while one-half teaspoonful of Karo likewise added may induce her to drink the milk-egg mixture as most dogs like sweets. In sickness we use strong jellied beef with raw egg yolk beaten into it in cases where the milk-egg mixture does not agree.

For the other two meals give one tablespoonful finely cut raw beef or underdone cooked beef or hamburger mixed with a little whole wheat crumbs. This, with two saucers of milk makes a perfect diet for the first week. Continue the milk if the bitch will take it, plus two saucers of a mixed-meat combination, any kind of easily digested beef, lamb, heart, kidney, chicken or liver. A little liver, lightly cooked and mashed into one of the other meats, will tempt even the fussiest feeder to consume the entire meal.

Sometimes a matron turns out to be a shy feeder around the third day after whelping. Especially if the litter is large, she must be induced to eat, otherwise the milk and egg mixture will have to be force-fed until she eats of her own accord. Roasted heart and kidney, or liver seared in a little butter will usually tempt any female to eat, unless of course, she is infected and is running a temperature.

As a general rule, for the normal bitch, provide milk or any type of milk pudding for the first few meals, then raw or lightly cooked meat, mixed with cooked egg noodles or buttered toast crumbs, or fish boiled in milk, exercising great care to remove all bones. Soft-boiled egg and buttered toast crumbs, in fact, anything highly nourishing and easy to digest will be satisfactory.

The lactating matron should have plenty of good muscle meat plus organ meats if her puppies are to thrive and have correct bone composition. Raw beef is considered about the easiest on the digestion; it is a natural food and should be given as soon as possible. While the puppies are nursing we feed no vegetables except tomato juice poured over commercial biscuit, if these are used, and we alternate tomato juice or broth or milk to pour over the biscuit before mixing the meat and biscuit together. Do not rely on meat broth as a real nourisher; actually it is more of a stimulant for the digestive juices than a food unless prepared in a very special manner. However, broth does have its place as a softener of kibbled biscuit though we do not regard it of much value otherwise.

When raw beef is fed in conjunction with kibble, it is recommended that the kibbled biscuit stand at least twenty-five minutes to take up whatever liquid is used for moistening, whether it be broth or milk; milk, of course, being our first choice. When the mother is about ready to wean her family, vegetables may be added to the diet. Tomatoes, onions, cooked mashed carrots, raw cabbage and stringless green beans are all useful and suitable.

Should the dam be infected and running a temperature, she may be unwilling to eat, hence, must be force-fed four times daily. For the purpose, use the raw egg and milk mixture, or jellied broth and egg, or any of the commercial beef extracts added to milk or egg.

Liquid beef peptonoids, Bovril and preparations of the kind are satisfactory. If not seriously infected, the matron may be tempted to take a few nibbles of solid food by dropping choice pieces of heart, kidney, liver or beef on the blanket in her basket, or even directly on the puppies. Instinctively she desires to keep puppies and basket clean so she eats the morsels more to get them out of the way than because she actually wants them; but the end result is the same.

When despite all tempting she refuses to eat and has to be force-fed with liquids, we avail ourselves of the special, tablespoon-size feeding spoon, or the old standby, the eye dropper. Fortunately, medicine droppers called ascepo syringes, now come with glass barrels of tablespoonful capacity; they are more easily cleaned than the old-fashioned small droppers and require less time as they hold so much more.

Occasionally when running a high temperature, the matron vomits solid food, in which case she will require the help of the veterinarian who may administer penicillin shots and saline or glucose solution. At any rate, in such serious cases it is wise to have a foster mother ready to take over the task of puppy feeding. Foster mothers are not always easy to find when needed. Insert an ad in the local paper, or seek out other kennels housing small breeds to ascertain whether a foster mother can be rented. Or, if a mongrel happens to be available, pay to chloroform her puppies (all, save perhaps one or two), and arrange to transport her to the scene of difficulty at once. Years ago, before the age of penicillin and modern drugs, we lost quite a few bitches whelping, but we raised their litters successfully on cat foster mothers as well as on Beagles, terriers and small mongrels. These days when the matron is infected, the good veterinarian can usually save her if he is called in time.

Right here let me say that no one raising dogs, even the house-pet owner, should be without a rectal thermometer and a knowledge of how to use it. The dog's normal temperature by rectum is 101°, and any rise from the normal indicates trouble. Immediately after whelping, the first in-rush of the milk can cause a slight rise of temperature to 102° the second day. This is not alarming, but anything over that requires immediate attention.

For reducing the temperature, use penicillin, given in one hypodermic injection, it will last twenty-four hours. With the penicillin we use sulfathiazole tablets, every few hours, in the number of grains as directed by the veterinarian. If this is done in time, the bitch can be saved, unless the uterus has been torn or punctured by instrumental delivery and septic poisoning is well advanced. Should the infection trace to a retained afterbirth, and the bitch be in good condition otherwise, and strong, she may be able to fight the infection, and with the help of the mentioned drugs, plus intelligent care, recover. If she lives beyond the fifth day there is every chance of a favorable outcome. A warning: If stilbestrol is used to clean out the uterus when an afterbirth is retained, this drug may dry up her milk. It has happened here, so if it is necessary to use stilbestrol be prepared for supplementary feeding. Keep the puppies with her as they will try to nurse, and their suction may bring the milk back. Also, nurse them if possible on another mother, or use "Esbilac" formula and feed with a medicine dropper.

Tulyar sired many champions including Ch. Tul Tuo, Chinaman and Ch. Tul Ku Zac of Orchard Hill.

Ch. Tul Tuo of Alderbourne.

9

Care of Young Puppies

THE litter at three weeks has reached a milestone in its development when several innovations in the care of both mother and young will be in order. Rather startling changes will have been noted in the growth of the puppies during these first three weeks. How rapidly they have come along from somewhat shapeless little moles, born blind and helpless, their four feet strong enough merely to push plump bellies along the floor, their instinct nothing more than the desire to nurse and cuddle up against the warm body of their dam! At ten days or so they opened their eyes but as yet they did not see; they had ears too but the brain was not ready to do much about the interpretation of sound.

All this is now changed, for the puppy is developing at an amazing rate, not so much as regards actual size though that too is increasing, but mostly as regards sight and hearing and mental awareness, physical motility and the first sign of a desire for cleanliness. The eyes have lost their bluish baby stare and begin to sparkle darkly, while the more precocious of the colony make tremendous effort to get up on their feet. With a mighty heave, up they stand, sway drunkenly and sit down, only to try again and again to support their own weight on all fours.

Direction is not one of their strong points when first they begin to walk or run, or balance either. They are more reckless than human babies; they fling themselves about just for the joy of making themselves go, and they may head for one corner and end up in another. At any rate, with surprising facility they learn to navigate around the box. They tip up, fall over and push, and in the process strengthen their legs. The instinctive massaging of the breasts with their feet as they nurse may even scratch the matron with fast growing, pin-point nails. Their nails should be carefully cut to prevent eye injuries that often lead to ulceration and marked eyes.

The dam also requires a bit of extra care both for her own comfort and for the ultimate safety of the puppies. She has been sticking rather closely to her job, though after the second week her whole-souled enthusiasm has lost some of its fire. Each day finds her willing to spend longer periods away from her puppies; we see her stealing quietly out of the box while the babies sleep, to take her own siesta on the floor. This is as it should be, an instinctive and very gradual separation which is for the best interests of all concerned. The female is not neglecting her brood; her growing reluctance as time goes on to return to them is nature's warning that the little ones must shortly be on their own.

When the puppies are three weeks of age, the box front is removed and layers of newspaper are laid on the box-floor and a small blanket kept on one side so that the puppies will crawl to the paper and seldom soil the blanket. In really cold weather, or if the puppies are not doing well, we keep the box-lid down especially at night, and use the electric pad on low heat in the under-floor compartment. As the youngsters grow and get up on their legs, they will attempt to climb over the eight-inch front. At four weeks we encourage more exercise, giving the puppies the run of the pen by removing the high front while the mother is outside.

We now start weaning by keeping the mother away during the better part of the day though returning her to the babies occasionally during those first few days. We then keep her from the puppies until about 6 P.M. when she can look after them through the night. At times when the boxfront is left off, close down the lid thus ensuring a safe perch for the dam to jump on to escape from the puppies; or better still, place in the compartment a get-away bench low enough for her to scale, but too high for the nipple-hungry youngsters to reach and pester her. If a puppy is flat chested, not able to get up properly on its legs, use a piece of carpet in the pen instead of slippery newspaper. These washable rough carpet samples can be bought anywhere and help the puppy to get up, and when legs get traction and exercise it is possible the chest will fill out.

At four weeks of age each puppy is given twice daily at 8 A.M. and 4 P.M. raw scraped beef, in amount about the size of a large pea. With a silver knife scrape *with* the meat grain so that the pulp is detached from the connective tissue. We moisten the meat with a few drops of cod liver oil, then gently force tiny bits into each puppy's mouth to induce chewing. Usually the puppies take it well; the oil keeps it from adhering to the roof of the mouth and of course serves a medicinal purpose as well.

In the presence of weak legs, flat chest or any apparent deficiency in bone we provide additional vitamins in oil, ordinarily using the A.B.D.E.C. drops made by Parke Davis for human babies. The dose is one drop on the tongue just before the scraped beef and cod liver oil mixture is fed. The amount of scraped beef is gradually increased until at six weeks a full teaspoon is taken, while the weak puppies have their vitamin drops increased to two drops at each meat feeding.

At five weeks we teach lapping. For the purpose we use a special glass dish, a heavy non-tippable chick-feeding saucer with raised center and narrow circular avenue around it for the milk. This makes a wonderful puppy dish. The youngsters cannot upset it, clamber into it or push it about; they can lap without spilling and getting themselves bedraggled. We use it for our weaning formula as well as for water drinking. Our milk formula which is a special one given me years ago by Dr. Edwin Blamey in New York is superior to anything we have tried, and it is suitable also for a sick dog.

Formula: Mix the yolk of a fresh egg in a cup with one teaspoon of lime water and one-half teaspoon of Squibbs sugar of milk. To this add one cup of Grade A whole milk. Mix well, store in the refrigerator and use as required. Warm to body temperature enough of the mixture for each puppy (about two teaspoonfuls per puppy at the start) and pour into the feeding dish.

Some breeders make short work of the initial lapping lesson by the simple expedient of pushing the little face into the milk, but that is not the best method to employ with short noses. Instead we follow the age-old calf-starter practice of dipping the finger in the milk, letting the puppy lick it off and as he does so we guide his tongue by means of the finger right down into the dish. He soon acquires the art of lapping, and in the process is less apt to daub up his face.

At this age milk should comprise two meals and meat two meals, the specific hour for the four-meal daily routine depending somewhat on the owner's personal convenience. Here we feed meat at 8 A.M., the milk mixture at 11 A.M., meat again at 3 P.M. and the milk mixture at 6 P.M., when the mother is put back with the litter for the night.

At eight weeks the entire egg is used in the milk mixture, the dam is kept away entirely and an extra dish of plain whole milk is left with the puppies throughout the night. Now the afternoon meal can be made up of lightly cooked beef, ground, and variety and amount increased. Egg noodles cooked in meat broth can be added to the ground beef, or the meat can be supplemented with other suitable starches like well cooked barley or rice; or whole wheat toasted bread, or one of the better commercial baby foods or commercial puppy foods. There are in fact any number of good ones that are suited for use at this age provided enough meat forms the base.

Where dog biscuit are used, make sure the manufacturer guarantees that no preservative such as formaldehyde has been added—I know of several kennels whose dogs developed running fits after being fed on a well known make of kibbled biscuit. It is safer, therefore, in my opinion, to stick to home-cooked cereals and baby foods when feeding young puppies.

For the owner of the house pet, or the breeder keeping just a few dogs, the commercial canned baby meats, also the junior chopped canned meats will be found useful and if purchased in quantity lots will prove no more expensive than fresh meats. These make an ideal diet when fed in conjunction with a little whole wheat toast to absorb the juices. If canned foods of the sort comprise a part of the

Ch. Ku Chi of Caversham won 32 CC, sired many champions.

Ch. Caversham Ku Ku of Yam, 7 times Best in Show all-breed championship shows. Holds the breed's all time record of 39 CC. Sire of many champions. Son of Ch. Ku Chi above.

Ch. Ku Jin of Caversham, well-known sire of English and American champions, by Ch. Caversham Ku Ku of Yam, owned by Mary de Pledge.

menu it is advisable to give raw hamburger as one of the two daily meat meals.

These small cans of liver soup, chopped lamb, etc., are excellent to have on hand as an invalid food or for emergency rations; they are equally advantageous to take along to dog shows or when travelling anywhere off the beaten path when fresh meat may be unavailable or difficult to purchase. And for those who attend shows, a can opener and a box of kibbled biscuit are a grand solution of the feeding problem for one can will provide two meals for an 8-pound dog.

The two-months-old puppy is now on his own. He can have the run of a small, sunny pen with access to an open-air runway. Daily he should be given his two meat meals, two milk meals plus the small saucer of plain milk left in the pen for the night. This last milk feeding is not altogether necessary, but it does help to form good bone and sturdy legs; and incidentally, the natural calcium thus derived from the milk is better by far than all the tonics and tablets put out for the purpose.

There are times when one feels justified in retaining a weak-boned puppy because of the value of its bloodlines or its place in a planned breeding program. For the building up of these, such commercial preparations as Pervinal, and the number of others, will be found effective. However, as I advised previously if a puppy of this kind has been given the A.B.D.E.C. drops, plus cod liver oil on the raw beef, also lime water in the milk, such added sources of calcium and vitamins are seldom needed. Vitamins from natural sources like liver and other organ meats, muscle meat, whole milk and eggs, tomato juice, orange juice, some raw vegetables, etc., together with intelligent management will build the sturdy, heavy-boned, sound legs that the standard demands.

The three-months-old puppy is now ready to be wormed and subsequently transferred to a new home unless he is to be retained as a show or breeding prospect. Here at Orchard Hill we do not worm puppies younger than three months, for we learned years ago to worm every dam previous to her mating. This worm-free condition of the dams, plus meticulous cleanliness of houses and yards makes the incidence of worms a rarity in our puppies. If before being mated a bitch is checked microscopically for worms by the veterinarian, and then wormed if necessary, her litter will be worm-free provided any worm infested excretions she may have passed are deeply buried or burned.

Even so, as an added precaution we worm puppies at three months of age, using a mild worm capsule; and if any worms are forthcoming we repeat the dose in three weeks and never again thereafter unless definite evidence shows up in fecal examinations. Under the microscope the veterinarian can detect worms and worm eggs in a small amount of the feces and, having determined the exact type of internal parasite, he can prescribe the right drug in the correct dosage for the patient at hand.

Where grass or dirt runways are used, there is constant danger of bringing in hook worms, either from a visiting bitch or from the introduction of new dogs to the kennel. Thus a yearly examination of the feces is advisable as part of the regular routine. Hook worms, which can cause hemorrhage and death from ulceration of the intestinal walls, are almost impossible for the layman to detect; even on post mortem they are hard to see, consequently the yearly checkup of all dogs in the kennel is a wise precaution against the spread of this killer.

Clean runways are vital if worm infestation is to be avoided or at least held to a minimum. Excretions of wormy dogs that are exercised on grass or dirt should be dug up, limed, and then buried deeply elsewhere. Here, we have concrete runs which are cleaned and hosed daily, and in the summer frequently disinfected with strong salt water to kill both worms and worm eggs. The feces are shoveled up, bucketed and burned, after which all runways are hosed into gutter and drain.

At four months, the extra saucer of milk may be omitted and three daily meals given. Breakfast consists of raw ground beef with a teaspoonful of cod liver oil over it. We advise feeding the beef raw at this time in an effort to circumvent the quite usual young-puppy preference for cooked meat. When hungry from the night's fast, the little ones will readily take the raw beef which their rapid growth demands.

The next meal, at noon, can be made up of whole milk over any dry breakfast cereal, or over pablum or any guaranteed puppy biscuit. Or, the noon meal may consist of home-made milk pudding which all puppies love—cup custard, bread pudding, corn starch, rice pudding, junket and things of that sort.

The third meal or supper should include meat such as cooked beef, lamb, heart, kidney, liver, chicken, fresh pork or a canned meat—never feed horse meat to puppies. Whichever type of meat is used for this meal, it should be mixed with a suitable starch and a small amount of vegetables such as tomato, mashed cooked carrot, onion, string beans, or raw finely shredded cabbage. If the meat is boiled, noodles, macaroni, barley or rice can be cooked in the broth, then added to the meat and vegetables.

After the meat has been run through the grinder or finely cut, the supper should consist of three quarters meat, one quarter starch and vegetable, while any broth left can be used next day to pour over kibbled puppy biscuit and a roasted meat used. Except for milk, we never use soupy mixtures, hence this supper should be fed in crumbly, rather than sloppy, consistency. Its quantity will depend upon the age, size and activity of each dog. The puppy of four months will need a tablespoon of raw beef for one meal, and the same amount of cooked meat with a teaspoonful of vegetable plus two of a starchy food.

Bones also are beneficial at this time, not only as playthings, but to assist the teeth as well. Round steak bones, knuckle bones or flat rib bones are the proper kind, but never a steak or chop bone that can be splintered. Bones serve as pacifiers for the youngster whose gums swell and grow sore from the imminence of changing teeth. Constant gnawing helps to loosen and break out the milk or baby teeth and it may possibly play some role in the prevention of tartar in older dogs.

At six months the puppy can be given two meals per day, the same as outlined for the younger puppy, but with the quantity increased and the hours changed to 8 A.M. and 4 P.M. If milk is enjoyed, it should be given at supper time. Here we feed milk regularly in the evening to every dog that likes it. If the puppy is now doing well and in good flesh, the cod liver oil is omitted.

Whether the puppies are to be retained for breeding and showing, or whether they are to be disposed of to new homes, each should be registered with the American Kennel Club. Of course, the litter must be registered to make way for the registration of the individuals.

As far as registration of the individual is concerned, it is advisable to wait until the puppy is three months of age, for colors change and it is frequently embarrassing to register a puppy as fawn-colored at two months only to have it turn into a red at four months. Strong colors can be determined at three months, the blacks for instance and the deeper reds; but lighter reds, fawns and sables are difficult to figure out with certainty, so for these the deferred registration is preferable. Otherwise, the new owner may request a corrected registration certificate when the fawn youngster finally emerges as a red.

Miss Charleen Prescott sent me an interesting article she had in Pekingese Parade on "Loss of Puppies Due to Enlarged Thymus Gland," and wrote, "I am pleased that you want to use the Thymus Gland article in your book."

Loss of Puppies Due to Enlarged Thymus Gland

"Our recent experiences in saving two puppies from two separate litters may prove to be helpful to other breeders when faced with the same situation.

"Our first puppy, when 2½ weeks old, suddenly had trouble nursing—the milk gushed out through the nostrils. He became progressively weaker with labored breathing and spells of gasping and 'swimming' on his stomach. Our veterinarian, diagnosed the case as an enlarged thymus gland. We quote from Webster's Dictionary: 'Thymus: a ductless glandlike body, of undetermined function, situated in the upper thorax near the throat; it is most prominent at birth, after which it disappears or becomes vestigial; the thymus of an animal, when used as food, is called sweetbread.'

"Upon further research, we learned that an enlarged thymus may produce local pressure on the windpipe, esophagus, blood vessels and nerves, with the development of lack of oxygen in the blood; difficult or painful breathing; raspy sound in breathing due to obstruction; and extreme difficulty in swallowing.

"The condition of the enlarged thymus is often erroneously diagnosed as pneumonia or a deep cleft palate as the symptoms are similar. The most important symptom is moderate to severe difficulty in breathing, gasping and inability to nurse. Eventually, signs of blueness of the skin (especially noticeable in the tongue), weakness and malnutrition, loss of weight and dehydration may develop.

"Successful treatment was given our first sick puppy with X-ray therapy. After the first treatment, the puppy was fed with Esbilac administered through an eyedropper which was inserted in the side of the mouth and injected part way down the throat so the milk would not immediately emerge through the nostrils. After two days of feeding four times a day every five hours, he was able to suck on a nipple. However, the fourth day after the first treatment the symptoms reappeared, so back he went for another X-ray treatment. One day of feeding with an eyedropper gave him enough strength to nurse again, and the puppy was put back on the mother. He is now going on eleven weeks and is a normal, healthy little dog.

"A regular X-ray machine is used and the settings are 45 Kilovolts and 8 Milliamps for one minute at 25 Centimeters Distant. The Thymus does not shrink at birth in these puppies, but remains enlarged and causes breathing troubles. The X-ray shrinks it."

Ch. Ku Chi as a Chinese mandarin.

10

Feeding the Grown Dog

STRANGELY, many a newcomer to the ranks of toy breeders believes a small dog can be fed a little of this, a little of that without regard to the nourishing value of the tidbits provided. Under my constant questioning, beginners in dogs have come up with the most peculiar assortment of menus anyone could devise, the listings including a plethora of concoctions from brown bread to beans, and even commercial biscuit served dry in a trough! This is not fancy, but fact. And so I always take pains to explain our own method of feeding which has proved satisfactory through the years.

I advise beginners to learn as much about the principles of nutrition as they can in order to instill respect for the offices of the various foods and to bring home the fact that the toy requires the same basic nutrients as does the larger dog. Little or big, his growth processes are identical: to keep him growing, to make him strong and sturdy, he needs the proteins, the carbohydrates and fats, the minerals and vitamins. Plus water and air, these are the things he must have if he is to survive and grow as nature meant he should.

The first three are known as the organic substances. In the main, the proteins make the frame, while the carbohydrates, otherwise called the sugars and starches, together with the fats, produce the energy for activity or movement. In other words, the proteins build the body and the carbohydrates in conjunction with the fats make it go. Under certain conditions, of course, the offices of these three nutrient types can be interchanged, meaning that for a short time and through necessity the carbohydrates and fats can do the work of the proteins, but they cannot do it as well. To be specific, the dog deprived of his full quota of meat will not starve if fed starches and fats; he will grow after a fashion, but he will not grow as well nor will he be as resistant to disease. He has only that much to grow on left over after his energy requirements have been satisfied.

Of both plant and animal origin, proteins are present in meat, fish, egg, milk and milk products, and certain cereals. Those of animal origin are preferable because they are more complete as to their amino acids while the cereal-derived proteins are seldom complete. Moreover, in dog feeding, proteins of animal source are preferable because the dog is a carnivore or meat eater hence thrives on a larger proportion of meat than does man. The carbohydrates are found in such foods as bread, macaroni, rice and other cereals as well as in some of the root vegetables. Like the proteins, the fats too derive from both plant and animal sources and include meat, fish and vegetable fats and oils.

With perhaps a few exceptions we find in the enumerations above just about all the things a Pekingese needs, not however solely because they are proteins, carbohydrates and fats, but because they incorporate the inorganic substances as well, namely, those accessory food factors or regulators we call minerals and vitamins without which life and growth cannot continue. One reason why the wild dog was able to subsist on an all-meat diet was because he ate small game in its entirety, that is, the muscle flesh and the liver, heart, kidney, etc., the last named three, or glandular organs, containing the regulators which the muscle meat lacked.

The minerals are highly important, contributing to the feeding scheme a longer list of benefits than it is necessary to detail. Twelve or more are required by the body, many in 'trace' or infinitesimal amount, others in comparatively larger quantities. The trace minerals we need not worry about for the average dog will get his share;

but in perhaps four—calcium, phosphorus, iron and iodine—his diet may be deficient.

The good offices of calcium are legion. Suffice it to say for the limits of this article that it forms a part of the bones and the teeth, and that it aids the productivity of the female. During pregnancy and lactation more is required than at any other time in the animal's existence, with considerable amounts obligatory for growth of the young, and somewhat lesser amounts for maintenance of the adult. Sources include milk and its products, cheese, eggs and greens, fish, beans, peas, etc.

Phosphorus is linked up with calcium and hence is as necessary because it works best in conjunction with it, assisting in the formation of bones and teeth, the building of the cells and alkalinity of the blood. Fish, liver, barley and wheat, brown rice, cheese and milk, beans and peas are likely sources which should be on the regular menu of the pregnant and lactating bitch especially.

Iron is needed in no great amount, but needed nevertheless, for deficiency may lead to the serious anemias. It is found in a wide range of foods—veal, pork and lamb, liver, heart and kidney, spinach, kale and beet, and many more.

The iodine requirement, too, is not great in amount though vital. Its lack predisposes among other things to flabby musculature, poor coat and generally unsatisfactory growth. Its principal sources are drinking water and foods raised along the shore as well as in other soils naturally rich in it. Those raising dogs in known goitre belts have used with excellent effect iodized salt as a lightly sprinkled seasoning.

Vitamins are a complex subject that I think need not be discussed in any great detail here. Since their comparatively recent discovery their number, kind and myriad good offices have been brought to light at a tremendous rate; they have been lettered and numbered, grouped, divided and subdivided until nobody knows how many more lie in the offing ready to be found and ticketed as to their specific services.

They are not foods in the ordinary meaning of the term; they are food accessories which serve as protectives against subnormal functioning, and they interact with the minerals. Best of all names that have been applied to them is regulators, for in truth they play a part in regulating such processes as growth, reproduction and lactation.

They serve the eyes, the skin, the appetite, the blood; in fact, careful study of the work performed by the vitamins as known today leaves scarcely any portion of the body unaffected by their influence.

The various vitamins, too, in themselves are interacting, perhaps that is why we find different vitamins in the same foods. And we find them in so many foods that the dog given a sensibly varied menu day after day is practically certain to get his share, provided of course the foods are fed fresh.

Vitamin lists, each with its specific reference to sources in which it is normally found, discloses that the following foods rank high in one or more of the necessary vitamins:

Milk	Liver	Fish
Butter	Heart	Fish Liver Oils
Buttermilk	Kidney	Vegetable Oils
Cream	Muscle Beef	Tomatoes
Cheese	Pork	Carrots
Egg Yolk	Chicken	Leafy Green Vegetables
	Whole Grain Cereals	

The dog fed these things, and fed them fresh, is a lucky dog for he will grow strong and well; and rarely will his owner be called upon to worry about the state of his health or the size of his veterinary bills. The trouble with dog feeding in the past was that it tended to become too stereotyped, too restricted in its variety. Today we know the dog can eat with benefit just about everything man eats. As a general rule, we do not feed potatoes or pastry or nuts, and we do feed him proportionately more meat than man eats. Otherwise, we turn him loose on the whole bill of fare, even to fruit if he likes it.

Meat may comprise one-half of the daily diet, and this we feed both raw and cooked. Though raw meat is the dog's natural food, domestication has robbed him of a certain amount of his instinctive liking for it. Quite early in his career the tiny puppy learns to snap up eagerly bits of raw beef, but later on, when he has been given an opportunity to sample cooked beef, he often prefers it to beef in its natural state. So when a dog grows choosy as to the kind of meat and the method in which it is served, we fool him by compounding his dish of a variety of meats, a little of it raw, a little cooked; some cooked muscle meat, some kidney and heart, fresh boiled tripe, etc., at different feedings. And when the meat lacks fat, we always add raw suet.

Where horse or whale meat is used for grown dogs, fat in the form of raw suet is extremely important, for this type of meat is notably fat deficient and if fed without the addition of fat may cause acidity, scratching and loss of coat. Never feed horse meat to puppies. When fed to grown dogs, alternate with beef.

By the popular expression that fat is needed to burn up the starches we mean simply this: Though fat is required for its energy and vitamin value, it works best when given in conjunction with the starches. Which once more points up the body's need for the big three—proteins, fats, and carbohydrates—for balance. A balanced cooked meal may consist of muscle meat, organ meat, fat, some starchy food or biscuit plus raw cabbage or other vegetable cooked.

According to modern dog nutritionists the dog's 24-hour food intake should contain a minimum of ten percent fat. It is easy to insure the necessary amount if the food is measured by tablespoons. For example, the dog consuming two tablespoons of food in twenty-four hours will require in addition one teaspoon of finely minced suet. It is better to use slightly more than the minimum amount rather than not enough; at the same time, do not overdo it for the average dog, as fat is considerably more of a digestive job than anything else. Furthermore, do not melt the fat; it may possibly hinder digestibility in some cases, and it renders the food mass sticky which is one of the things to be avoided.

Fat in the diet, which among other things aids coat growth and prevents skin irritations, can be supplied most economically in the form of suet. It is not too expensive and with deep freezers and locker plants available it can be purchased cheaper in quantity. And while considering the cost of feeding, it is well to point out that heart, kidney, various other types of meat and suet may be found cheaper on certain days when they can be purchased and frozen for later use.

Dog owners and breeders located within reasonable distance of a fish market by all means should feed fish once or twice weekly. Most Pekingese relish fish boiled in milk or water for a change, but make sure all bones are carefully removed. One's finger tips are the only safe guide to fish bones, some of which are so small and so perfectly color-matched with the flesh as to escape detection otherwise.

Certain tiny fish bones too are little more than cartilage, at least they are not rigid; at the same time even these constitute a hazard for small dogs that had best not be risked. After cooking, drain the fish in a colander (saving the liquid for combining with the starch or cereal component of the meal), then pick over the flesh with the fingers to search out the bones.

Eggs are very important in the diet, but they must be clean eggs. Make sure they are thoroughly washed before cracking or your puppy or grown dog may get that dreaded coccidiosis. It is often fatal and resembles distemper in a way. The very loose bowels are caused by parasites from the egg shell from chickens infested with coccidiosis and if the shell has any dirt spots on it from a fouled hen's nest thoroughly scrub or discard it. We had this disease in my kennel years ago from using dirty farm eggs and we lost a number of promising puppies. They died from severe and uncontrollable diarrhea. If the shells are cracked, the only safe way to use such eggs, is to hard boil them.

Eggs in any form are good alone or they can be added to the dog's regular dish. They are of special benefit to stud dogs and to the bitch in whelp. For force-feeding picky eaters and poor doers they are invaluable. It's a simple matter to spoon into the mouth the raw yolk so rich in fat and the fat-soluble vitamins. Poached and combined with buttered whole wheat toast or shredded wheat they make a highly enjoyable meal.

In conclusion about what to feed, some dogs, like some people, invariably have good appetites and will eat anything. These are what we call good doers. Others, to make satisfactory progress, must have special things, more tempting mixtures. Common sense and good judgment on the part of the kennel owner are required in the handling of poor doers which often get along better if placed in private homes where variety table scraps and individual attention will fatten them up.

One hard and fast rule in our kennel is never to feed the dogs anything unfit for human consumption. Good fresh foods will prove more expensive, but they pay in the end as carefully raised dogs are undoubtedly more resistant to disease hence live more comfortably, more happily, and they do not require the expenditure of so much for drugs and veterinary services.

As to the quantity of food given, I admit we are not too hidebound

Head study of Hindley Taylor's San Fee of Kyratown.

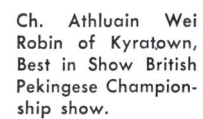

Ch. Athluain Wei Robin of Kyratown, Best in Show British Pekingese Championship show.

Ch. Kyratown Lu Tong of Redstock, greatest winning Pekingese bitch of all time.

in this respect. Doubtless the ultimate in scientific accuracy demands that we feed exactly so many ounces to the dog in this compartment, so many ounces to that dog over there, and so on. Here, we skirt around the weight bogie with surprising facility and, I make haste to add, practicability, by knowing how much our feed pans hold, namely, a *full* measuring cup (not a teacup); meaning four ounces of meat and four ounces of filler such as biscuit or other starch and vegetable. If perchance we err one way or the other, the dog himself will advise us by means of his actual condition. The breeder soon grows expert in judging a dog's state of flesh, his activity and nervous stability, when more or less can be fed.

But when I say more or less, I mean that the balance or component parts of the meal, to a greater extent than the overall quantity, is changed to suit each individual requirement. For example, when we come to bitches in whelp and nursing, and for thin dogs and studs used heavily, instead of the 50-50 combination we feed more meat and less filler, or ¾ cup of meat and ¼ cup filler, fed twice daily depending on the size and appetite of the dog. Some bitches that are inclined to grow too fat are given one meal of raw meat alone, in quantity at least eight ounces for an eight-pound dog, then the second meal of the mentioned cupful is composed of half meat, half filler.

In general, the ordinary kennel dog, one year of age and weighing ten pounds, is fed a minimum of eight ounces of food daily, plus milk if he likes it. But when feeding the same dogs day after day, we do not feel guilty in neglecting exact weights and measurements for we soon recognize and provide for individual idiosyncracies. We see one dog definitely eating too much for his own good, another not eating enough; we note a certain dog as making better use of the amount offered him, while another of perhaps the same age and body weight does not utilize his food to the same extent and thus must be fed a larger amount.

When all is said and done, the meat portion of the meal is its most vital component and this should not be stinted. Many house pets are what we call "sleeves" or miniatures and these, of course, require usually about half as much food as specimens of standard size; but even a sleeve weighing in the neighborhood of four pounds should consume four ounces of meat per day plus some filler, milk, etc.

Aside from the quality and quantity of foodstuffs given the dog is the method of serving it. As far as the Pekingese is concerned, method is particularly important. His muzzle is short, and broad, therefore he cannot comfortably reach into a deep dish. Even if he could, there exists every probability of daubing up ear fringes and face cushion.

For grown dogs we use aluminum pans, six inches in size and only as deep as an ordinary pie plate. These can be purchased at any hardware store, I believe they are made for baking small individual pies. For puppies from three to six months we use the same type of pan in $4\frac{1}{2}$-inch dimension. All pans are washed with soap and water, then scalded, after each feeding and stacked compactly on a handy shelf in readiness for the next meal.

Above our inside pens we have cages so that dogs which have a tendency to fight, or which may require special diet, may be fed each one by himself in a separate enclosure. In fact, I think all dogs are better fed separately. In this way, proper check can be made as to whether the dog polishes his plate, whether he picks and chooses or whether he is off-feed entirely. The dog fed alone has no opportunity to scuffle with his fellows while the greedy one cannot get more than his share at the expense of the more deliberate eater.

One bothersome phase of feeding concerns perpetual dampness of compartment flooring as a result of water splashed from drinking pans, this being particularly prevalent in summer when buildings are not artificially heated. The subject was touched upon earlier in connection with puppies, but it applies likewise to many adult dogs so frisky that they never seem to grow up. They regard water not alone as something to drink, but something to play with so, in an excess of spirits, they wade in if they can or upset the container and strew the water about. For puppies, and in certain of our grown-dog pens, we use the quart-size galvanized chicken fountains which are difficult to overturn and which feed into the surrounding saucer only a small circle of water for lapping.

11

Diseases and Nursing

A chapter of this kind could be written at great length if the subject were to be covered in its entirety. But as numerous books have dealt adequately with first-aid treatments, a repetition is not needed here, and so I will give merely our own kennel routine for handling certain diseases common to Pekingese.

Whether a breeder assumes complete responsibility for the care of his dogs in illness, or whether he elects to work under the direction of his veterinarian, as time goes on he invariably devises methods of his own for treating his little patients, and he sticks to these methods because of their long-proven efficacy. Nursing remains much the same though the availability and administration of drugs differ from practices of only a few short years ago. Our dogs are, therefore, fortunate in having science come so ably to their assistance.

Topping the list of dogdom's ills, of course, is distemper. Years ago, I lost thirty-five Pekingese in a single epidemic. Mothers with nursing puppies, some older dogs and practically all my young stock died from enteritis, pneumonia and meningitis, each of these being a form of distemper. Such an experience is unheard of in these days when preventive inoculation against distemper can be given; and even when inoculation of the kind does not provide perfect immunity to every dog, it does do so to about 90 percent, and it lessens the severity of the disease for the few dogs not immunized.

Here is just one case to prove my point. All of our entries at a certain show some years ago had been inoculated; all those at home had been inoculated also except one puppy which I thought too young for the complete three-shot method used in those days. This puppy was isolated on our return from the show, and for one week everything was apparently all right. Then two of the show-goers developed eye trouble, head colds, loose bowels and a rise of temperature.

Only four dogs out of thirty that had been inoculated came down with distemper, and these four were off-feed and sick for only one week. We administered sulfadiazine for the intestinal tract, together with proper eye treatment after which they recovered rapidly. Somehow, the isolated puppy, only six weeks old, contracted the disease and died in four days. We gave him serum, but it was too late; meningitis developed and killed him quickly. Had the preventive serum been given to this puppy preceding the show or directly upon our return, I believe he might have been saved.

I doubt whether it is humanly possible to isolate a dog absolutely when kept on the same premises with distemper sufferers. In some unexplainable manner the germs travel about despite the strictest quarantine. Perhaps they are air-borne; at any rate, I have never known an isolated dog to *escape* the malady no matter how careful one may be to protect him. The sole safeguard nature apparently offers against distemper is in immunizing new-born puppies, provided the dam had had distemper and the puppies are nursing and have been given no other food. When left with the mother, not handled or weaned, there is an immunity set up in the milk which keeps them safely until protective serum can be administered at weaning age.

Pekingese are subject to respiratory ailments, and as distemper frequently takes that form, the ensuing pneumonia is usually fatal.

I insist on using only vaccines tested by Cornell Research Institute, and made by reliable firms such as Pitman Moore or Lederle. A certain vaccine was used by a veterinarian to inoculate twelve 3-month-old puppies against distemper hepatitis and leptospirosis. They all had bad reactions, one losing his eyesight, others had ulcerated eyes that left bad scar tissue, impaired vision and were ruined for show purposes. Perhaps some new vaccines are not suitable for dogs with full eyes, such as Pekingese and Pugs. The doctor tried unsuccessfully to collect damage claims for the dogs that were ruined. He now relies on Pitman Moore and Lederle's Tissue Vac DH, or CAB-VAC, one-shot inoculation to prevent distemper and hepatitis. He inoculates puppies at three months and later gives "booster" shots that are especially needed for young show dogs.

Research is constantly in progress and many breed clubs, as well as individuals, send yearly contributions to the Veterinary Virus Research Institute at Cornell University, Ithaca, New York. All breeders are urged to contribute; even a dollar helps. I am sure tears will come to your eyes when you remember how hard you tried to save a beloved one, to no avail. Remember even our *best* inoculations are not *always* effective. With new diseases so prevalent now, we have gone back to our old method of show protection. Wipe the show cage with a cloth and disinfectant, then before and after the dog leaves the ring dip each foot into a small saucer of rubbing alcohol. Also wipe nose and mouth with cotton wet with an antiseptic mouth wash. Infections are picked up through the nose, mouth and foot pads.

Some veterinarians prefer other types of vaccination, and cases and breeds may differ in their reaction. I write the above as personal experience only, but I am confident our method has stood the test of time. We attend most shows where distemper germs are always lurking and where in former years we invariably brought the disease home.

In treating Pekingese for distemper, serum has its value, and the sulfa drugs may save many dogs if used in time, but the disease is best combatted if it is recognized before too great damage has been done, and then careful nursing given. The secondary invaders—pneumonia is one—are the real killers, hence if distemper is detected early, the temperature checked and prompt measures taken toward control of the disease, many cases can be saved.

Probably the most vital need of the distemper sufferer is hospitalization in a room of equally warm temperature. Under no circumstances should he be allowed out of doors. Provide fresh air from a partially raised window in an adjoining room to guard against any semblance of draft or chill. In the presence of cold and head symptoms (running eyes and nose) make a woolen pneumonia jacket and tie it on securely. Apply Vicks salve to the nose and throat unless some other chest applications are ordered by the attending veterinarian, and administer the proper sulfa drugs. Brain cases and meningitis are hopeless and can be treated only by means of sedatives.

A few tips on feeding Pekingese in distemper may prove of value to someone. The following foods we have used successfully. For derangement of the bowels, or enteritis, try boiled milk thickened with arrowroot, Robinson's Patent Barley gruel as made for babies, with beef blood added to the gruel. Also beneficial is raw egg white, and plain beef juice squeezed with a meat press from lightly panned beef, or mix one tablespoonful of beef blood with one of barley gruel. These liquids can be force-fed every four hours. If the dog is very weak, or vomiting, try feeding small amounts every hour with an eye dropper. Also handy for force-feeding is an Asepto syringe. It is like an eye dropper only much larger and has a blunt opening and a round rubber bulb at other end. Liquid or semi-liquid food is easily forced out by squeezing the bulb.

A cupful of liquid food in 24 hours is sufficient to prevent dehydration, and if the fluids exert a binding effect plus their strengthening quality, a very sick dog can be nursed over that critical period. Canned baby foods also "Esbilac" are helpful and convenient. Very soft binding foods include corn starch pudding, junket or the yolk of a hard-boiled egg mashed, and small amounts placed in the patient's mouth. The bismuth preparations, as well as the old standard intestinal antiseptics can be tried in mild cases, but in the presence of serous enteritis and symptoms of pneumonia the veterinarian should be relied on to prescribe the modern sulfa or penicillin treatments.

In pneumonia cases where the bowels are not involved, the puppy-weaning mixture of raw egg yolk and milk is easily digested and quite strengthening due to the nourishment in the egg. Where the need for stimulation is apparent, add 5 to 10 drops of brandy and force-feed every four hours, giving from one to two tablespoons per feeding.

If the mouth is sore and the patient difficult to feed, use a small rubber ear syringe with soft rubber end or the Asepto syringe mentioned; wash the syringe thoroughly in hot soapy water after each feeding and let stand in a bowl of water to which a pinch of soda has been added.

In the presence of only mild symptoms, when the dog may eat of his own accord, there is nothing superior to finely cut or scraped raw beef given in small amounts, progressing as the case improves to ground beef in frequent tiny meals just as one would feed a very young puppy. Pablum and milk as another meal is also very nourishing. Then gradually work the patient back to his regular diet.

The all-important thing to keep in mind is this: Distemper is the dog's most serious disease, of long or fairly long duration. The veterinarian should be called when the first suspicious symptom is noted and his directions followed to the letter. Dig in for a real siege, for even in the presence of apparent improvement, anything may happen. Turn night into day; nursing is a 24-hour job, but faithful nursing pays off handsomely.

Another quite common Pekingese ailment, which we treat as a form of autointoxication, is popularly known as "going down on the hind legs." This condition we alleviate by giving a large initial dose of milk of magnesia—one tablespoon for a grown dog—followed in an hour by repeated doses of uratropin. Of the latter, one-half of a 5-grain tablet is thoroughly crushed in 1½ tablespoons of water, and given every eight hours until fifteen grains or three tablets are given in 48 hours. A teaspoonful of milk of magnesia is given each morning, but the uratropin is discontinued after fifteen grains are used. After a few days, if the patient is still semi-paralyzed, repeat as before. The uratropin is an intestinal antiseptic as well as a urinary antiseptic so if the kidneys are involved it is the proper medicine for the condition. Mixing breakfast bran, instead of biscuit, with the meat is beneficial. The patient must be kept warm. Heat applied across the back in the region of the kidneys helps. Massage of the hind legs is also indicated. In some cases where the kidneys are not functioning properly, a counter irritant is frequently prescribed by the veterinarian and applied as directed over the kidney area. Shots of Prednesone, 10 to 12 milligrams every third day, also 2 milligrams Prednesone Tablets once a day may be ordered by your veterinarian.

Stone in the bladder, too, is not unusual in bitches and unless very small must be surgically removed. Symptoms include frequent urination, a small amount at a time, often with blood in it, and straining without result. X-rays will detect the stone, when removal is imperative or the female may die from uremic poisoning.

Ch. Pu Chi of Chyanchy, bred and owned by Mrs. Lily Sawyer.

Bodkin of Drakehurst, homebred winner of many Bests in Show, owned by Mrs. Lillian Drake.

Ch. Linsown Ku Che Pet, Best in Show winner, bred and owned by Mrs. Y. Pownall.

Eye trouble is prevalent in the breed due to some extent to the prominence given the eyeball by the shallow socket in which it lies. Many beautiful dogs have lost their chance of gaining championship honors because of unsightly eye scars. Whether they trace to internal or external causes, permanent injury can in numerous instances be prevented if morning eye inspection is made a regular practice and treatment promptly administered at the first indication of that blinking stage. An entire chapter might be writen on the Pekingese eye, but space does not permit, so only a few remedies will be mentioned.

Blinking, with an aversion to strong light, is the first sign of trouble when an examination may disclose a tiny dent or hole on the surface which is the beginning of corneal ulcer. At the start the indentation is infinitesimal and difficult to detect. Over night the eye may turn a bluish, milky color. Three or four times daily, wash the eye with sterile saline solution, thoroughly flushing out any accumulated matter by holding the lid away from the eyeball and gently squeezing an eye-dropperful of the lukewarm solution over the surface. Then when clean, use the correct eye salve or other suitable medication. We have had good results with sulfathiazole eye salve, in fact, we prefer it to penicillin on account of its longer lasting potency and freshness. If the trouble is detected and treatment administered before serious ulceration sets in, this salve will effect a cure, with only a small scar or perhaps none at all resulting. One percent Atropine Ointment is also very good. If used twice daily it will keep the pupil dilated and the retina from scarring.

In former years we used argyrol of various strengths, and sometimes yellow oxide of mercury salve, also zinc preparations—an entire medicine chest could be filled with eye remedies. We have tried them all and find that some eyes respond successfully to one kind of drug, some to another. On the whole the sulfathiazole salve seems a more reliable remedy, easy to apply. It does not pigment the eye as argyrol may do in the presence of definite indentation. While argyrol is a good antiseptic, its prolonged use has a drying effect on the eyeball unless applied in conjunction with vaseline, while the pigmentation sometimes brought about may result in blindness.

From the very start the dog must be kept in semi-darkness or at least out of strong light; likewise, he must be prevented from rubbing the injured eye and thus causing further damage. Cocaine (2%) dropped into the eye every four hours for the first twenty-four hours will allay the pain, while a stiff cardboard collar, made Elizabethan style, will make it impossible for the dog to scratch the eye with his foot. The most dreaded condition, staphyloma, develops when the inflammation breaks down the cornea allowing the inner layers of the eye to protrude. Expert veterinary care is required for, if the fluids of the eye are lost, blindness and a shrunken eyeball are inevitable.

Newer eye salves in use now that we find effective in many cases are Schering's Eye Ointment Metimyd with Neomycin. White's Vitamin A and D salve is very good when an ulcer is healing. Use once or twice daily. When treating an ulcer, "keep the hands cleaner than clean," as other dog's eyes will become infected if even a trace of pus gets in them. Do *not* use Cortisone, as it has a tendency to "set" a scar.

In my opinion, eye cases differ and different treatments are indicated in almost every case. We get more eye ulceration now because of more overnose wrinkles. The heavier hair of the modern wrinkle often touches the eyeball causing irritation and unless the heavy wrinkle is trained, that is the hair kept pressed together by pressing the wrinkle between the thumb and forefinger, the irritated eye will ulcerate. Wrinkle training should be a daily job. Some extra heavy wrinkles need special care. These are helped by using curved nail scissors. Lightly trim the outer edges of the wrinkle, the hair that can touch the eyeball. An assistant must hold the dog while the one using the scissors holds each eyelid down when trimming that side of the wrinkle. Before the modern eye salves, we relied on hot compresses as first aid. I prevented an eye ulcer from forming on a famous import at a critical time in her show career. The day before she became an Int. Champion, a blue eye developed. I made two cups of boric acid solution in a small enamel pan. I kept two gauze 2-inch-square pads in the hot solution on low heat and sat there with Ku-Rai on my lap for two-hour periods interchanging and holding those compresses on her eye. The blue eye cleared in 24 hours. Mrs. Herbert Mapes, one of our best-known exhibitors of those days, told me about saving eyes and advised the use of atropine sulfate for ulcers to keep the eye layers working and dilating so as not to adhere and make scar tissue. I must quote Mrs. Harp's novel experience when her dog, later a champion, was turned down because of slight eye scars to a light-eyed dog. The Harp dog had dark eyes as our standard requires. The judge whispered to her, "You know those scars might be *permanent.*" It just dawned on Mrs. Harp, perhaps the judge thought the light eyes were *not* permanent.

Here, ear canker is unknown; nevertheless, it is prevalent in some kennels and can be detected at many a show on otherwise well cared for dogs. Frequently, visiting bitches arrive suffering with it, whereupon their owner are told one of our kennel secrets. Years ago I was told by an old time breeder how to prevent canker and since then we have never had a case. Twice each week while in the process of grooming, every dog's ears are cleaned with *dry* cotton and after all folds are carefully gone over, a pinch of dry boric acid powder is dropped into each ear. Shake ear leather gently so powder dusts all crevices. Just as simple as that! And, I might add, so much easier than attempting to cure a case. Canker is extremely painful to the dog and when neglected for even a short time is practically impossible to cure permanently, hence prevention is very worthwhile. Be suspicious of the dog that frequently scratches an ear, or that carries his head tilted. Continual itchiness is an early sign; pain comes later when the dog may rub his head along the floor and whine or cry.

A fairly long list of causes might be cited for skin trouble, one of the more usual ones, in my opinion, being improper diet. Where the diet is not at fault, scratching and sore spots are usually occasioned by fleas or other external parasites, or by a fungus condition resulting from lying in damp places, or from grass runs. There are a number of good skin remedies, among them the old fashioned "mange cures," such as Sanahide, Kur Mange, etc., which seem to take care of minor skin eruptions. Milk of magnesia given internally, and applied externally to summer "hot spots" is worth a trial, but as I have already said in connection with feeding, there will be far less skin trouble if enough suet or fat is included in the diet. In this discussion I am not referring to such serious skin afflictions as ringworm and follicular mange—these are in an entirely different category, requiring sterner measures and veterinary advice.

A good dip formula for a fungus condition is 6 ounces of dry lime sulphur to one gallon of warm water. Put cotton in the dog's ears. Use a foot tub and have lots of newspapers on the floor. Do the head first, being careful to protect the eyes. If pure vaseline is smeared around the eyes and lids it will prevent any dip from getting in them. Wear rubber gloves if hands are sensitive. Sponge and wet the dog all over. Squeeze off excess water, but do *not* rub him dry. Let him *shake* himself dry on the newspapers. This dip and self-drying must be done in a warm room. Do not allow the dog outside until the next day.

A breeder asked how to get rid of fleas and ticks. We do not have that problem here because our runways are concrete and the dogs do not run in grass or shrubbery where fleas and ticks hide. Our runways are hosed down daily into drains and the big maple trees at the end of the runways furnish shade and do not harbor ticks. The only fleas we get, or ticks, are picked up from grass show rings or from show dogs in competition with us. Dogs must be carefully inspected on arrival home from a show, removing any fleas or ticks before they are put back with their kennel mates. Pulvex and other powders are efficient, but for ticks be sure the head is removed or a festering sore will result. A good method for removing ticks is to touch them with alcohol. A cotton swab is good for this. Use fingers or tweezers and they come away easily, head and all. In using flea powders do the head first and by hand remove any that may be there, then dust the powder all around the neck so they cannot run back to the head, being careful of the eyes; then dust the body.

The breeder who asked about ticks described her runways. They are gravel surfaced. She is lucky indeed that so far none of her dogs have eaten gravel! I consider gravel or pebbles very dangerous for runways. I know of a Peke which died on the operating table from bowel obstruction and perforation from swallowing stones. Puppies especially pick up everything and anything either to eat or to play with and while gravel runs may be all right for big dogs, do not use them for Pekes. For some breeds, gravel runs are used to strengthen feet to prevent splay foot. We do not have that trouble with Pekingese. Concrete runs are good for their feet. They keep toenails short and wear off excessive toe fringes, and they are easily disinfected, which is so important in a hepatitis scare. Feces are easily picked up and burned and urine, a source of infection, is hosed down the drains. We often use salt solution for washing runways. It is a mild disinfectant and is healing for feet especially when there are sores between the toes.

Another warning!!! Never exercise your dogs on lawns that have been fertilized and sprayed. Insecticides and some fertilizers are dangerous not only to people, but to animals. I am not a Rachel Carson, but I hate insecticides as much as she did. If dogs run on lawns so treated they get these poisons on their feet. They lick their paws and scratch and thereby set up skin trouble and if much poison is licked there may be serious internal upsets.

Other summer pests are wasps and bees. They like to build their nests under the sheltered eves of kennel buildings. Watch out for them and be sure they are burned and destroyed as stings can be serious especially if in the mouth or on the tongue. If possible, extract the sting with tweezers, then swab out the mouth with bicarbonate of soda. For stings on the face or feet, apply soda or vinegar, then use an ice cap to reduce the swelling.

Oftentimes the breeder's medicine chest discloses a conglomeration of preparations recently, and not so recently, advertised until he grows so confused that he hardly knows which remedy to use and for what ailment. As far as the average breeder is concerned there are comparatively few drugs and household remedies he will be in a position to administer with safe and satisfactory results. However, these few he should keep on hand for use in minor emergencies.

Our own medicine chest contains a rectal thermometer, and castor oil which serves countless purposes. Aside from its office as an effective purgative, it is soothing to the skin, and very healing for anal abscesses, keeping them open and draining until healed. We also stock mineral oil, milk of magnesia, Uratropin tablets, aspirin, aromatic spirits of ammonia, brandy, alcohol, KY jelly, pure vaseline, boracic acid powder for ears, Vicks salve, glycerine and honey in equal parts to use for coughs; cornstarch for stops as well as puddings! Also eye salves, sterile cotton, bismuth subnitrate, Kaopectate for gastric irritation, plus most of the sulfa tablets now used for treating many forms of infection, Johnson's Baby Powder for grooming, a stock bottle of saline solution for cleaning eyes. A small eye dropper bottle is kept filled with this salt solution and used as needed for flushing out hair and matter from the eyes. The deep stop of a Peke, under the nose wrinkle, is often wet; the dog perspires through the nose leather. Formerly, we used boric acid powder to keep the stop dry. Boric acid is a poison and if licked often can do harm; use cornstarch powder instead.

12

Grooming for Home and Show Ring

EXPERT preparation for the show ring plays an important part in any dog's successful career; not that grooming can blind the connoisseur to faults but rather because it does help to make the most of a dog's good points. The most highly prized features of the show dog, of course, are breed type and body structure. Even when he excels in these, however, he must be properly put down if he is to get anywhere at all in competition with dogs of equally commendable conformation.

But what must always remain an enigma to those of us who take our dogs to the shows is why so few pet owners groom their dogs expertly for the home. The importance of a good general appearance cannot be over-estimated, and as far as the Pekingese is concerned, the coat is the first phase of general appearance that attracts the eye. True, the connoisseur can go down under the hair and pick flaws right and left, but the average observer, the home folks, cannot. Consequently, to the pet owner and his noncritical friends, the coat exerts a tremendous influence in any dog's favorable acceptance or the reverse. When we consider how comparatively few are the show dogs in proportion to the number of lesser lights going into private homes, we can appreciate the office of the pet as publicist of a breed.

This wide divergence in coat care I believe is the reason why many a breeder, regardless of the price obtained, would rather sell to a fellow breeder than to a pet owner; the breeder keeps the dog in tip top show-shape whereas the average pet owner may keep him clean but that is about all. The latter usually washes the daylights out of the coat, brushes it sporadically and combs out the tangles with a heavy hand. The result—a potential star that looks like a ragamuffin. And so I repeatedly advise every owner of a Pekingese to learn all he possibly can about grooming and to practice assiduously what he learns.

Good health is the keystone of good grooming; without it, the dog cannot strike that determined, somewhat aggressive attitude so characteristic of the Pekingese. Unless he be in perfect health he cannot grow that luxuriant coat which in kind and quantity and manner of stand-offishness attracts attention to him as king of the toys. For the coat is nature's final touch; she builds up the body strength first and then proceeds to put on the coat in amount and texture as directed by heredity.

The first requisite, then, toward good grooming is to have the dog in the acme of physical condition, clean inside and out. This means, specifically, freedom from internal parasites like worms, freedom from external parasites like fleas and lice, any one of which can nullify one's bet efforts to promote tiptop condition. Worms among other things upset the stomach and rob the vitality while fleas and lice irritate nervously and wreck skin and coat mechanically.

Throughout the life of the dog, the coat has its constant ups and downs, remaining in full bloom of quantity and color at various periods for a comparatively short time. It grows in, slowly reaches its peak then fades and sheds out to make way for the new crop. The young puppy coat is no more than a furry fuzz devoid of heft and durability, but about midway to maturity it begins to assume its characteristic two-ply texture, that is, a close-to-the-skin undercoat, soft and fine for warmth and skin protection, and a coarser, heavier overcoat for beauty and weather resistance. Normally, the coat is cast in quantity twice each year; in addition, a certain amount of shedding goes on all the time, frequently to so small a degree as to be scarcely noticeable.

Rarely does the young dog's coat attain full bloom until complete maturity at twelve or fourteen months. Following serious diseases like distemper the coat is ruined for the time being; what strength the dog has left is needed for recuperation, so none is available for any coat worthy of the name. As a result of whelping and rearing, the matron sheds deplorably, really goes naked and it is some time before her returning vigor is sufficient to raise a new crop of hair.

For the stiff competition of the show room, the coat should be in its full bloom of luxuriance and color depth; that is why many a show has to be skipped because the dog is out of coat. Of course, judges often make due allowance for out-of-coat condition especially in summer; but, be a dog ever so perfect otherwise, his lack of coat is sure to militate against him where an equally good specimen *in coat* competes in the same class.

The pet is not called upon to meet the severe test of expert coat appraisal. Even so, around the house, about the town wherever he goes he is under constant surveillance so he should look his best in coat and out. And he will be far more comfortable too as a result of faithful grooming. Whatever his status or quality, whether a beloved stay-at-home or competitive star, his grooming is identical. Only when the dog passes the portals of the show room does his grooming become more complicated, when the exhibitor gives those final touches just prior to entry into the ring.

Of what does correct grooming consist? First of all, common sense washing which means that the Pekingese should not be bathed too often. Some authorities on hair contend that long hair ought never to be washed with water at all, but this seems too rigid a prohibition. A certain amount of overall washing is needed, but never more frequently than several times during summer's hot weather unless the dog is especially soiled under the tail. Never wash the Peke just before a show, as the coat will lose its resiliency and lie flat, and never wash a female that is well along in whelp. All dogs, puppies especially, are subject to chill while being bathed so young ones under a year had best not be washed at all; the latter can be drycleaned with powder if necessary, or finger-massaged with a sprinkling of non-oily hair tonic. Many dogs of mine have never had a bath. Correct daily grooming keeps them perfectly clean.

If you *must* wash your dog, do it this way. In a warm, draftproof room stand him in a small foot tub filled just a few inches deep with warm, not hot, water. Wet the coat thoroughly with the clear water, then apply mild soap, preferably liquid, and rub it with the fingers down to the skin making sure to miss no part *except the face*. Do not risk soap in the eyes as it will irritate. Then, rinse well, three or four times if need be to remove every particle of the soap. Rub patiently with turkish towels and keep the dog in a sunny, draft-free place until completely dry. Rotary motion is more effective for drying, it also prevents breaking the hair which quite commonly occurs under too vigorous massaging against the trend of growth while the hair is wet.

Second, selection of the right tools. Avoid the sharp-needled wire hairbrush as the undercoat must be protected; it is the mattress on which the outer coat lies, and without this buffer the outer coat falls flat to the skin, hence loses its characteristic stand-off or wind-blown appearance. Care of the undercoat has to do with the selection of the comb as well. Many steel combs have sharp, rough edges that will catch and pull the precious hair! The only safe comb is the one with smooth teeth set a little farther apart than those of the ordinary steel comb. A fine steel flea comb is wonderful for shaping and grooming the overnose wrinkle.

Third, daily brushing and combing, and I mean *daily*. The need for faithful regularity in brushing and combing cannot be over estimated. In practically every kennel housing long-haired dogs, a certain hour or hours are set apart each day for this necessary routine, and there is no reason in the world why the house pet should not be accorded like service. There would be fewer hairs on the furniture if they were brushed out daily as they begin to loosen. Advisedly I put brushing before combing because that is the way it should be done. Brush first every section of the body, the ears, the tail, to separate each hair and to stimulate the circulation by the massaging action on the skin. If the dog has a long plume, make the most of it by keeping it brushed forward on the back, that is, toward the head especially where the body coat may be lacking. Then comb carefully, gently removing any tangles which the brush has not succeeded in straightening out.

Fourth, attention to the eyes. For the Pekingese, daily eye care is as important as daily brushing. In the presence of the slightest weeping or accumulation of matter in the inside corners, wipe the corners ever so gently with cotton dampened in sterile saline solution. Boracic acid is a poison and if the dog licks much of it, there may be trouble. Saline solution in a dropper bottle can be purchased at drug stores, and is safer to use for routine eye care. The stop under the wrinkle must be kept dry by using cotton. When dry, a pinch of cornstarch helps and is safer than boric acid powder, as if licked it does no harm, in fact they all love the flavor!

Fifth, while a relatively minor point, still has its bearing upon good general appearance, and this entails selection of the right collar and leash. The Pekingese ought never wear a flat collar; in fact, around the house the fluffiness of his mane will be protected if he wears no collar at all. Out on the street, of course, and in the show room, a collar is obligatory. Choose a collar made and stitched rounded rather than flat, and as small in circumference as reckoned necessary for strength. Devoid of straight edges, the round collar reduces to a minimum wear on the neck-ruff, and it is inconspicuous as a collar should be, because the mane can be fluffed up around it. The leash, too, should be as light in weight as is commensurate with safety. For the show ring get the thin, round silk-cord lead. The light-weight leash exerts no drag upon the neck which is important.

Let us assume that we have already given the aspirant for show honors this type of care and equipment, and that we are now arrived at the show.

We have with us a large thermos bottle of our local water; this is important these days as a change of water may cause diarrhea. One bowl is used for drinking water, another for grooming water. Several small hand towels and a wash cloth are needed. Cotton, eye lotion, powder are also in the show kit plus a hair spray. A good one that we use, is "Happy Hair Conditioner" with lanolin made by Caryl Richards. My hair dresser gets it for us. For hot weather shows be sure and include in your ice chest not only the dog's food, but plastic bags filled with ice cubes that can be refilled, and may be the important factor in saving your dog from a heat stroke. Rubber bands will keep the bags from leaking, and such a bag serves as an ice cap when applied to the head; and a towel wet with ice water will also bring relief if the dog is placed on it. Another point to remember—many dogs, other than short-nosed breeds, have died in summer when left in a car with the windows closed. This has happened at shows as well as in parking lots. Lock doors, but always leave *all* windows down at least six inches and park in the shade.

Now as to show grooming, the dog must be brushed first and any tangles carefully separated. Then with the cloth wrung from the bowl of water, we rub him vigorously all over to dampen the hair right down to the skin. While the coat is still damp, work into it with fingers a good talcum powder, exerting great care lest it get into the eyes. Do this about one hour before it is time to go into the ring. Return the dog to his basket or cage and about twenty minutes before judging time, start brushing the powder out of the damp coat. Pay particular attention to the ear fringes and the tail plume, and keep more powder and more dampness in places which may need help.

In this manner we are setting the hair as it dries, that is, we are manipulating it in such a way as to encourage it to take the desired trend. If the ears are a bit low-set, encourage the erectness of the aigrette (those hairs growing on the highest portion of the ear flap at the juncture of the ear with the skull); try to keep them up by back-combing the underpart and fluffing out the outside hair with additional powder. Comb the hair on the muzzle forward to widen its appearance. Brush the skirts downward. Make sure the eyes are clear of matter, and at the last moment with a clean, damp cloth wipe the powder from the mask. If, throughout this procedure, the hair becomes dry, dampen again with the sprayer of coat dressing to fluff up any places needing a lift.

Removal of the powder from the coat is as important as putting it in, perhaps more so in view of the AKC rule demanding that "such cleaning substances are to be removed before the dog enters the ring. If in the judge's opinion any substance has been used to alter or change the natural color or shade of natural color or natural markings of a dog, then in such event the judge shall withhold any and all awards."

The idea behind this rule is that powder may be used as a cleaning agent but not as a coloring agent designed to deceive the judge. When powder is used as I have described it for Pekingese, there is no attempt to disguise the dog in any manner but merely to clean and encourage the coat's natural growth trend. However, in obedience to the rule as it stands, the exhibitor should see to it that no vestige of powder remains in the coat when the dog enters the ring else it may be disqualified.

The suggestions regarding the use of powder apply to show room grooming only; for house-pet or for ordinary kennel grooming omit the powder as its *daily* use would prove too drying. Use it in the kennel to keep dry "skirts" under the tail where they have to be washed.

Another feature I should mention in connection with show preparation is care of the feet. The Pekingese has the characteristic hare foot which covers more ground because at least one of its digits is longer. It is, or should be, just as compact, as close-toed and arched as the shorter cat foot. Even when the hare foot is properly arched its length lends a deceptive air of flatness especially when further elongated by fringing. Actually it is not flat, but merely seems so. Therefore, the only way to enhance the appearance of the strong, well knit foot is to discourage too profuse toe fringing.

Pekingese feet are usually well fringed; however, very long fringes which might perhaps be suitable for Palace pets spoil the appearance of the modern dog by making the feet look as if down on the pastern. Concrete runs and adequate exercise will serve to keep the fringes short. The concrete wears the nails short also, keeps the foot pads firm and the toes close. And it strengthens pasterns and legs as well.

Development of strength in feet and legs is extremely important in a low-slung breed like the Pekingese. His body is heavy in proportion to his overall size, his bone is big for a toy, hence he has considerable weight to carry. The dog run on concrete or similar firm footing shows clearly the benefits of exercise; never does he exhibit that long toe-fringed look associated with the cushion and the lap dog.

13

Colors and Color Breeding

To most of us breeding for color in Pekingese is not important. We breed for type, color being secondary. Here and abroad we have a few specialists who are trying to produce whites and blacks, but no breeder of my acquaintance is willing to spend the long years of study that would be involved in producing a strain of, say, reds or particolors. They would have to go back ten generations at least to note the color of each ancestor; to ascertain the proportion of sun reds, particolors, and so on, in order to arrive at some sort of plan for their matings. This might have been possible when Pekingese were first produced but as it is now I doubt whether anyone could live long enough to own a breeding kennel of just sun reds or particolors. The usual pedigree has all colors in its background and all colors are permitted by our standard.

A few breeders have concentrated on whites or blacks with some success but it is frustrating, for even in the best planned matings off-color whites, black and tans, and sables do occur. Whites with off-color dudley noses, fawns, etc., lacking pigmentation, are proof that not enough blacks existed back in the pedigrees.

Novices may not understand the importance of using blacks in our breeding plans, not because we want to raise *black* Pekingese, but because we want to keep our colors strong. I have bred one hundred and fifty-odd champions including many blacks with good coats of correct texture. My first American-bred champion, Han Chuan, was out of the black English show bitch, Cleetonia Melita, the granddam of my famous 4½-pound Ch. Pier Simba, the little red male which was the sensation of his day. He was best of winners at the specialty and at Westminster where I refused five thousand dollars for him. This was a really big price for a dog in those days. The Herald Tribune had a box write-up about him—"Owner refuses a $1,000 a pound for a Pekingese!"

My first black champion was Fei Mina. When bred to Ch. Der Kai Shek, a red by Tri-Ch. Remenham Derrie, she produced Ch. Der Mina Mao, a red, and dam of many champions. Int. Ch. Sandee of Hesketh was out of Ayrtoon Pyxie, a black. Ch. Grey Spider of Hesketh imported by me, and her sister, Ch. Tulluah, were sired by black Ch. Cumbala Mejhas. My fawn Ch. Kho Yas Mins' sire was black Cameo Hei Chu Tzu. Mrs. Michael Van Buren owned lovely Ch. Pier Wan Li, a small typical black bred at Orchard Hill. My imported black Ch. Lo Yen was the dam of Ch. Pier Fei Sal, and on the Coast, Fernray Inkspot was the dam of a famous winner Ch. Major Mite of Honan. Our red Ch. Shangs Salle, winner of best of breed at our summer specialty some years ago, was by Pepper of Pekestone, a very good black. He sired four red champions including Ch. Jai Nie of Orchard Hill. Our black show bitch, Fei Tom Jemina is the dam of Ch. Kai Lung's Gem, a fawn winner owned by Bettina Belmont Ward. Our Ch. Pu Chi's Nubia was best opposite sex at the summer specialty. Black Jai Son's Anora was the dam of red Ch. Tulo Yu Chuo, best of breed at the winter specialty in 1956 and 1957. Anora was also the dam of two other champions, one red and the other fawn. The Misses Lowther owned Ch. Coal Dust which in turn sired Ch. Silver Dust, the sire of Ch. Silver Star. Silver Dust's daughter, Ch. Black Dust, had two lovely daughters, Ch. Black Diamond and Ch. Black Pearl, both noted for their correct stand-off coats. In a letter to me, Miss Lowther said, "I do think blacks are needed as we attribute velvety black masks to them." Another profusely coated black on the Coast was Mrs. Gene Hahlin's Ch. Chia Lee of Han Lin, the sire of many champions. Mrs. Mar-

Ch. Han Shihs Domino, owned by Mrs. Pearl Cassler.

Best Brace in show, Ch. Sin Dee and sister, Man De, black and tans by Jai Han Sung, shown by Gene Hahnlin for Grace Krieger.

Oliver of Wongville, owned by Mary Hilton.

jorie Nye Phulps was well known for her efforts on behalf of black Pekingese and an old letter of hers says, "Japeke Stormy's Dinah was the first jet black, American-bred champion bitch." Mrs. Phulps also bred Ch. Japeke Han Shih's Domino, the first all-black champion male. His sire was my light fawn Ch. S. Av. Hanshih.

Other famous blacks of the past were from Miss Higgs 'Yu Sen Kennels. I will quote now from Mary Whitelaw and Joe Higgs' article in *English Day World* concerning an American writer that did not like blacks. " 'Joe Higgs, the well known breeder and judge, has bred a large number of blacks in the many years he has been associated with the breed.' The American writer said that she only knew one black that had a good coat, and goes on to say, 'blacks have wavy curly coats with no undercoats.' " The indignant Mr. Higgs wrote, "Nearly all the Chinatown, Fen Yen Shang, Yu Sen and Bonrayes were black-bred and the Yu Sen blacks and their progeny produced the biggest percentage of post war winners both here and in America. In past years there were many famous black champions that sired champions (he names fifteen), all of which possessed the desired texture of coat. Both Ch. Yu Sen Yu Toi and his son, Tri Ch. Bonraye Fo Yu came from black dams and were black-bred for generations. These bitches carried true Pekingese coats and were winners. If their coats had not been correct, we would have seen poor texture of coat in later generations from them. I think it is only fair to the breeders of today that this article be challenged, as if it is read by novices here and in America, it would do infinite harm to the sale of black puppies and may also influence some judges who will think *all* blacks are poor and not wanted. I know how difficult it has been to get a black through to top honors." Mrs. Whitelaw goes on to say, "Blacks are very necessary to the breed and when used with reds, they help to fix a deeper red. I remember Yu Sen Christina. I saw her when Ch. Yu Toi was about two weeks old and little did I think he would become so famous! Christina was a very beautiful bitch and had many lovely children. Yu Toi was by Yu Sen Yu Chuo, the sire of Puff Ball of Chungking. Yu Toi was the sire of Ch. Bonraye Fo Yu red sable with black mask. He was never beaten in the puppy classes, then retired awhile and shown again at fifteen months and at his first four championship shows he won three challenge certificates and one reserve best of

Ch. Bonraye Fo Yu, champion of four countries, shown with Best in Show cup, Havana, presented by a cousin of Spain's last king.

Ch. Pedmore Cream Puff, lovely cream bought from Orchard Hill, owned by Mrs. I. Shallenberger.

Pai Toi Too of Roke, a good white, owned by Mrs. Marion Vegas.

Hallmark's Mr. Checkers, owned by Horace Wilhoite.

Ch. El Acre Sea Foam, owned and bred by Mrs. Longacre, the only white American bred champion in 1963.

sex, thus gaining his title. This is only one of the success stories of dogs whose ancestors or immediate parents are black."

Irene Miles is one of our pioneer breeders of blacks and a review of her Ir Ma Mi Kennels has already been given with an illustration of her black champion. She has done a lot of winning with her blacks and it is indeed good news when a black wins, since their brighter colored brethren so often catch the judge's eye. Black Pekingese and perhaps black Pugs do not have the color contrast, like the black masked fawns to bring out the intensity of their best points. It takes good judging by one who knows the standard, to evaluate properly black Pekes and Pugs and to give them their just desserts in the show ring.

One of the best black bitches I have seen is Ch. Black Queen of Orchard House. She was imported in whelp to Ch. Caversham Ku Ku of Yam by Mrs. Ward and is the dam of her famous Kow Kow. All of us who appreciate good blacks were delighted when Ch. Bettina's Kow Kow won Best in Show at our 1959 and 1960 Progressive All Toy event. The following year his dam, Ch. Black Queen was not only there to applaud her son's third victory, but was herself placed best of opposite sex to him. All of this proves the importance of using good blacks in our breeding plans, especially true for our reds and fawns.

I have never bred or owned a white Pekingese, but have judged some very good ones. Years ago a really top one was shown under me at Houston. This bitch Mei Lan of Bergum was owned by Elaine Bergum, then of Phoenix. She had no trouble gaining her title nor did her kennel-mate Lin Tu of Bergum.

The Sin Toy Kennels, located in Amarillo, Texas, were unique in the fact that they owned two white champions. Their English bitch was Ch. Yu Lana of Kaiwood, their American white champion, was Sin Toy White King. Both had dark eyes and black pigmentation; they were typical specimens of the breed. Pure whites with dark eyes and black noses are hard to breed unless most of the ancestors are white and have as well dark pigmentation. Color breeding in Pekingese is difficult to practice since all pedigrees have mixed colors behind them. None of the early dogs in England was all white; those that came later were from a combination of parti-color, fawns and creams, probably with a black or two in the mixture.

Faddists are in many fields, even in Pekingese breeding, and a recent rage, and to me quite appalling, are inquiries for blue puppies! I know what a "blue baby" is, but I have yet to see a blue Pekingese! Years ago, Miss C. Ashton Cross bred a dog that was "blue" and was later sold to a Dutch person for a very high price. Mrs. Walsh of the Celadon Pekes showed a bitch at Crufts some years ago that they say was a "true blue." A Shih Tzu exhibitor saw it at the show, and suggested that the color may have come from a crossing of the Tibetan breed of the Shih Tzu with Pekingese in China long ago. This blue bitch whose name is Copplestone Puck Nesta was bred by Mrs. Bentinck and sired by Copplestone Raven Phu, a black, out of Copplestone Puck Nessa, a red. Rose Marie Jenson of Medford, Oregon, is very much interested in raising "blues" and has been working on that problem for a long time. She wrote me, "I am not as yet ready to introduce the blues and I imagine it will be one or two years before I am ready to do so. When they are ready for new homes they will only be sold to certain breeders here in the States." I end this by saying, "Color doesn't count, teacher." It is type we want.

. and Am. Ch. Fu Yong of Jamestown, winner of 6 Challenge Certificates at 2 years old, a son of Ch. Jin of Caversham and Ch. Suzie Wong of Jamestown, imported and owned by Presleen Kennels, Ohio.

BODY heavy in front; not too long; females longer bodies

SIZE: extreme limit 14 lbs.

TAIL-SET high, lying over back to either side; long profuse straight feather

MUZZLE wrinkled, very short broad; not overshot or pointed

HINDLEGS lighter than forelegs, firm, well shaped

COAT long; undercoat thick, straight, flat; coarse but soft; feathering profuse

SKULL massive, broad, wide; flat between ears; wide between eyes

MANE profuse, forming ruff or frill; extending beyond shoulder blades

BACK level

RIBS well sprung

Quaint, individual; expression implies courage, boldness, self-esteem and combativeness rather than daintiness or delicacy

COLOR: all allowed including partis

EYES large, dark, prominent, round, lustrous

EARS heart-shaped, not set too high; not carried erect; long feathering, leather length not below muzzle

STOP deep

NOSE black, broad, very short, flat

JAW strong, broad underneath; teeth must not show

CHEST broad, falling away behind, lion-like

FORELEGS short; forearms' bones bowed; firm at shoulder; feather profuse

FEET flat; toes turned out, not round

14

Judging the Pekingese

OUR original standard has not been changed but judges do change, and some of the newer ones should study and re-study that standard. For instance, we count only 15 points for coat, feathering and condition. The Pekingese is what we call a "head" breed. We count 40 points out of the 100 total for flatness of skull, width of muzzle, eyes, etc. I do not mean to infer that a dog should win on head points alone, but I do believe some judges are influenced by coat and glamour, more than by body structure and correct head points. As for head points, many dogs today seem to be weak in underjaw with an "Andy Gump" mouth, instead of level lips.

While on the subject of the correct mouth, there has been considerable discussion and some protests from breeders who show Pekingese as to why some all-rounders open a Peke's mouth. All rounder judges of the past seldom did this and of course *no breeder-judge ever* opens the mouth unless it looks *wry*. If the tongue protrudes or the jaw seems wry, the judge can ask the handler to open the mouth, but why do so? This serious fault is self-evident and mouth opening is not necessary. A wide underjaw with level lips is also self-evident. The undershot jaw is necessary and helps to make the wide "kylin" mouth our standard calls for. Most serious fault is the overshot mouth with droopy upper lip. This too is easily seen, so mouth opening is not necessary. Pekingese resent having the mouth opened and it should not be done unless the mouth looks wry. Even lips and width of muzzle can be seen by all judges. A forced opening of the mouth can *break* the lower jaw and is not unusual. It is very easy to dislocate the lower jaw as in Pekes it is not a continuous bone, but two bones joined loosely in the center. If a mouth *must* be opened, the lower jaw must *never* be pulled down. This invites disaster. To open correctly, put fingers gently into the mouth corners and raise the *upper* jaw. Pekingese breeders do not consider it good judging practice to force open a mouth that is correctly formed.

My remarks on the prevalence of pinched nostrils was read by the English breeder, Mary Whitelaw and in her English *Dog World* column she says, "No breeder wants pushed-in noses or pinched nostrils, but they do come and, as the nose plays such an important part in proper functioning of the body, I feel this is a fault which must be tackled seriously. Short-faced breeds suffer in hot weather and their distress is increased if because of pinched nostrils they cannot breathe properly."

On the same subject, Irma Scheid of Bradenton, Florida wrote me as follows: "I do hope breeders will keep on emphasizing large *nose holes*. I recently bought a beautiful bitch, had her less than five weeks; she strangled, became frightened because she couldn't breathe and actually was "scared to death." Our doctor said her throat became frozen with fright. Isn't this a horrible thought that we are causing such things? I love the flat face, but I can see that especially in hot climates we must get back to more open nose holes."

Many dogs of today have too much wrinkle, some practically cover the nose leather and are so heavy one wonders how the dog can breathe. If Frances Mary Weaver and Mrs. Ashton Cross were here and saw these ultra-modern types, I wonder what their reactions would be.

But back to judging. I wish some of our judges could have attended an English party that was given by the London and Provincial Pekingese Club. A feature of the party was the lecture on judging given by Miss Marjorie Ashton Cross. This account, I believe was written by Mary Whitelaw in their *Dog World* column. "Miss

Ashton Cross gave a very clear description of the points of the breed and demonstrated on one of her own dogs just how the front legs of a Pekingese should *not* be. This dog was a very good example of concealed faults, having a huge coat and fringes, a real *trap* for the novice judge! It illustrated how the looseness of the front legs threw the whole body out of line, causing a rise at the back, which could be cleverly hidden by expert grooming. She also demonstrated how to make the best of a slightly round head (back roughing and fluffing up the ear fringe), and how to shorten a rather long back, I say 'rather' because a really long back cannot be hidden even by an expert. There is a trick too for the skirts which does quite a lot towards making a dog look well balanced."

With these all-over coats so prevalent in the show ring today, it is difficult to see the level back and body outline. If one stands behind the dog, looking towards the head, a proper pear-shaped body is easily seen, as the chest and front will project outside and beyond the hips. Dogs that are as wide across the hips as across the front do not have the lion-shaped body our standard calls for.

A breeder-judge who was trying to decide between two dogs of equal merits as to head points and legs had this to say about the loser. "It was difficult to decide between them, both worthy firsts, but the very profuse coat of the second place dog marred his body outline." We all want good coats and fringes, but not superfluous coats that completely hide the body shape. I would like to see judges pay more attention to conformation and balance especially width and depth of chest with great spring of ribs. Narrow chest and poor rib formation make the body "shelly," a serious fault in Pekingese and a hard one to breed out. Judges should handle the rib cage and thereby determine if conformation is correct. Some toy judges forget to feel the ribs and put a dog up on head points, coat and outward appearance. A good judge is able to evaluate the dog as a *whole*. He does not pick on one virtue or one fault to put a dog up or down. It is the all-over picture that counts. The breeder judge does not place a dog with light eyes over a dog with a slightly marked *dark* eye, the former a serious inherited fault, the latter an accident. The breeder judge does not put up a narrow jaw full of crowded teeth, also inherited, over a dog with correct muzzle, perhaps a few teeth missing from distemper, another accident, and not inherited. Nor does a good judge put up a straight-legged, narrow-fronted dog over the low bowed heavy legs that may be slightly out, the former a serious inherited fault, the latter a fault that can be bred out more easily. Finally, the judge who puts up the flashy "eye catcher," the soft-coated "bit of fluff" lacking correct body structure over the dog in fair coat of *correct* textures which does possess good ribs and body structure. These remarks are meant for novice judges, as doing our breed is a serious responsibility.

Of all the dogs in the toy group, Pekingese are the hardest to judge. The novice judge must first learn correct type and head points, then look for soundness, balance and gait, then coat, trimmings and show manners. This does take time and study. We desperately need young judges, those who are willing to give it that study. We who are old and experienced cannot last forever. Our regular judges are fair and try to do their best, but as I said before, it *is* a difficult breed to judge, the standard must be kept in mind, personal preferences forgotten, but do not forget it is a toy breed. So, the smaller dog all points being equal *can* win over a larger one.

STANDARD OF THE PEKINGESE

EXPRESSION: Must suggest the Chinese origin of the Pekingese in its quaintness and individuality, resemblance to the lion dog in directness and independence and should imply courage, boldness, self-esteem and combativeness rather than prettiness, daintiness or delicacy.

SKULL: Massive, broad, wide and flat between the ears (not dome-shaped), wide between the eyes.

NOSE: Black, broad, very short and flat.

EYES: Large, dark, prominent, round, lustrous.

STOP: Deep.

EARS: Heart shaped, not set too high, leather never long enough to come below the muzzle, nor carried erect, but rather drooping, long feather.

MUZZLE: Wrinkled, very short and broad, not overshot nor pointed. Strong, broad underjaw, teeth not to show.

SHAPE OF BODY: Heavy in front, well sprung ribs, broad chest, falling away lighter behind, lionlike. Back level. Not too long in body; allowance made for longer body in bitch.

LEGS: Short forelegs, bones of forearm bowed, firm at shoulder, hind legs lighter but firm and well shaped.

FEET: Flat, toes turned out, not round, should stand well up on feet, not on ankles.

ACTION: Fearless, free and strong, with slight roll.

COAT, FEATHER AND CONDITION: Long with thick undercoat, straight and flat, not curly nor wavy, rather coarse, but soft; feather on thighs, legs, tail and toes, long and profuse.

MANE: Profuse, extending beyond the shoulder blades forming ruff or frill around the neck.

COLOR: All colors are allowable. Red, fawn, black, black and tan sable, brindle, white, and particolor well defined. Black masks and spectacles around the eyes, with lines to ears are desirable.

Definition of a particolor Pekingese: The coloring of a particolored dog must be broken on the body. No large portion of any one color should exist. White should be shown on the saddle. A dog of any solid color with white feet and chest is *not* a particolor.

TAIL: Set high, lying well over back to either side; long profuse, straight feather.

SIZE: Being a toy dog, medium size preferred providing type and points are not sacrificed; extreme limit 14 pounds.

Penalization: Protruding tongue, badly blemished eye. Overshot and wry mouth.

Disqualifications: Dudley nose—Weight over 14 pounds.

Scale of Points

Expression	5	Shape of body	15
Skull	10	Legs and feet	15
Nose	5	Coat, feather & condition	15
Eyes	5	Tail	5
Stop	5	Action	10
Ears	5		
Muzzle	5	**TOTAL**	100

Illustrating perfect mouth, Ch. Pier Buzz of Orchard Hill.

15
Traveling by Car

WITH the expansion of the purebred industry, the number of dogs travelling by rail and by air increases day by day; even so, the larger share will doubtless be transported by auto. Most dogs nowadays are brought to the shows in their owners' cars, while the number of those annually crisscrossing the country, vacation bound with the family, is really incalculable. Therefore, it is but common sense to teach the dog to ride so that he will accept the auto as casually as he accepts his own home.

Such teaching is not at all difficult, but it is necessary for the simple reason that the dog reacts sometimes to unaccustomed motion by vomiting. Most Pekes adore to ride in the car and if started as puppies soon regard this mode of travel as a matter of course. If not started at an early age some become frightened and car-sick.

The initial trips had best be of short duration, and in moderate (never extremely hot) weather, with the puppy held in someone's arms to obviate the first discomfort caused by dip and sway. Do not leave the dog on the seat alone for his weight is not sufficient to hold him down against the force of sudden stops—if even once he goes sliding to the floor he may be hurt physically and he will surely be upset nervously. The first few short rides, taken on an empty stomach will almost without exception leave a pleasant impression on the puppy's mind, the sole black mark against the procedure being that thereafter it will be difficult to take the car out without him.

It is not unusual for breeders to administer a mild sedative to their dogs prior to a long motor trip in an effort to prevent car-sickness. They soon learn to be good travellers and if taken for short rides once a day for a week before any long trip is attempted, or if they are taken on shopping tours of the local stores, they quickly become accustomed to the motion of the car and suffer no ill effects. Feeding immediately before riding is frequently a cause of car-sickness, therefore, we never feed before starting on a trip. Usually we leave in the morning, then feed after reaching our destination. Allow the dogs to get settled first, after which they are watered, rested and fed in that order.

When transporting a carful of dogs to a show, we place at the back of the station wagon those accustomed to riding, while any lacking much car experience have their baskets back of the front seat, in case soiled or wet papers have to be removed. In each basket we place many thicknesses of newspapers, lifting off the top layers as may be required. We also carry with us a wire folding pen to set up on a grassy spot to exercise the dogs well before taking them into the motor court.

Since motels have been made so comfortable the past few years, we always try to find one along our line of travel at or near the show, in preference to a hotel, because these usually have grass plots and other better facilities for exercising than the more formal hostelries. Too, the privilege of parking the car right at the door or in the drive adjoining has its advantages. Many motor courts, and hotels too for that matter, nowadays welcome dogs; others do not, because some owners and handlers abuse the privilege and allow their dogs to jump on beds and do other serious damage.

When we stay at a motel, we keep the dogs in the bathroom in small folding wire pens, with newspapers on the floor, or we utilize a clothes closet where the floor is not carpeted; and across the door we erect a pull-out window screen of a height that cannot be jumped over. Screens of the kind, which can be purchased at any hardware store, can be used in the home for confining the pet in a closet or room, while four or five screens fastened together make an inexpensive, light-weight, movable puppy pen.

The new Safari wire crate made by R. Steele Company is fine for the purpose as it has a removable floor. It is safe for dogs in cars, it closes securely and is wonderful for hot weather shows, especially unbenched ones. They come in various sizes and are light-weight and easy to carry; ideal to use at a hot unbenched show, the floor can be removed and the dog can lie on cool grass.

We take along a supply of newspapers and a small suitcase with water dishes, little metal pans, a can opener if canned food is to be used, and a bag of dry, kibbled biscuit to mix with it. When we take fresh meat along, as we usually do, we roast beef hearts which, after cooling, we cut in quarters and freeze solid in a neat package. This we remove from the deep freeze just as we leave, and wrap in many thicknesses of newspaper. It remains frozen for hours. When ready to feed, we cut it into bite-size pieces. For this, scissors are preferable to a knife, consequently a pair of good kitchen scissors is always included in our travelling kit. Our dogs love juicy roast heart better than any other food; in fact, I find that most dogs of any breed, which do not eat well when on the road, will eat heart with avidity. It is the ideal food for dog show travelling! Occasionally we cook a little liver with the heart for special tempting though this is rarely necessary.

We also carry ice in a light-weight thermos case to keep the meat frozen. If several days supply is needed or if weather is very hot, it is safer to use canned meat. I discovered a new canned product on the shelf with other baby foods called Finger Food for Juniors; most supermarkets carry it. There are seven small meat sticks to a jar, a beef pork mixture, skinless, that the dogs love.

Water is another important item to be provided for when travelling. Should there be any question of the water supply, or when taking dogs from North to South where the water may be brackish, full of sulphur or other chemicals, it is advisable either to buy bottled spring water or to take along a thermos of home water. Many dogs develop diarrhea from a sudden change of water.

When sojourning at a motel we assure the management that our dogs were exercised upon arrival; that they will be confined to their baskets when we are not with them, and will be fed and watered on newspapers in the bathroom; in short, that no damage will be done to furniture, floors, woodwork or other appurtenances.

When leaving, we pick up every piece of newspaper, every bit of evidence that dogs have occupied the rooms. Uneaten food, hair, anything and everything that might point to our dogs' stay is taken from the place or, if more practicable, rolled and thrown into the waste can. Bedroom and bath are straightened up just as we would do in our own home.

There are two sides to this question of taking one's dog or dogs into strange quarters, be it hotel, motel or summer cottage. We all know that upon occasion such premises have been inexcusably abused. If all dog owners would leave temporary abodes as they found them, few such places would be barring dogs today.

Ch. Kai Lung of Vinedeau's as a puppy.

16

Shipping by Rail and Air

SHIPPING puppies to distant buyers is a hazard that all breeders must face at one time or another. While puppies sold within reasonable radius of one's kennel are usually called for and taken home by car, there are many which must be transported to their destination by rail or air.

Under the right auspices, the three-months-old youngster can be shipped; in fact, from a psychological standpoint the puppy of three or four months is apt to travel better than he would a bit later when nervously unstable by change of teeth and the natural demands of rapid growth. But if he is to travel in comfort and arrive in good condition, the dog of any age must be properly outfitted for the journey.

Shipping by rail is customary for comparatively short distances. Be sure the shipping crate is sturdy and large enough, strong but light in weight, and with a wire or grill door. We use rounded top, plywood crates equipped with a carrying handle at its center top. And if the weather is cold and the dog young, we cover the lower half of the grill door with cardboard which can easily be removed when the express car is hot or the weather happens to moderate. In view of the change of the seasons and the unpredictability of the weather, crates must be adapted to all kinds of temperatures—hot, cold and medium. And let it be remembered that foremost among shipping hazards is heat with lack of adequate ventilation. Smothering to death is not pleasant to contemplate, but it is worthwhile to keep it always in the forefront of our minds when preparing to send a dog on a journey all by himself. Looking the grim spectre right in the face pays dividends.

For hot weather use, our kennel man evolved a special summer shipping case by removing the sides from the regular rounded top fibre-board crates and substituting quarter-inch heavy aviary wire. This was bent to fit the frame from one side to the other, and nailed securely to the bottom of the sides and to the front piece where the metal door is hinged, also to the frame uprights. The front and back sections of the crate are left as they were. The result is a crate very light in weight yet sturdy enough for shipping and withal full ready to admit life-giving air in even the hottest weather.

The crate furnishings, too, are important. To the front corner of the crate is fastened with cord a removable tin cup so it cannot be upset. Do *not* place inside the crate one of those heavy china drinking dishes unattached. I have had bitches arrive here for breeding, lame and sore as a result of being hit time and again in transit by such dishes. Safer by far is the old-fashioned tin drinking cup tied to the crate handle or inside the door.

The crate floor is well filled with torn newspaper strips to provide a deep bed which will cover and at least partially absorb all excretions. The puppy, and the grown dog also, will reach its destination in better shape when bedded on torn paper than on flatlaid paper or blankets. We feed each prospective traveller a good meat dinner two or three hours before shipping, then we exercise him well to provide every opportunity for evacuation before placing him in the crate.

As for food en route, never send meat; the safest is non-spoiling dry stuff such as Milk Bone, Jr. biscuit. A bag of biscuits is tied securely to the crate handle. The dog will be fed by the express company attendant as directed by you on your shipping tag.

Be sure that the consignee's full name and complete address and phone number are plainly displayed. Most kennels use their own printed shipping tags as they give general instructions for care and, being blank on one side, allow space for the shipper to write the dog's name as well as any special directions plus an appeal for·the animal's welfare, such as, "I am gentle and will not bite. My *safe* arrival depends on *your* good care."

Before a dog is sent out, be certain he is in perfect physical condition. It is necessary to have one's veterinarian give a professional checkup and issue a written health certificate, also certificate giving dates of distemper, hepatitis, and rabies inoculations. Dogs in transit are usually insured at full value; and proof of perfect health upon departure is necessary in the event the dog arrives at his destination in anything except good health. It is also advisable to discuss the journey with the express agent or air line well in advance, principally to learn of possible strikes or embargoes affecting any states through which the dog may be routed, also to find out flight numbers and time of arrival so consignee can be notified.

As all of us who have shipped dogs to any extent know, the fast-growing modern method is transportation by air, and here too, crate ventilation assumes major importance. The famous English Ch. Yu Sen Yu Toi, for which I paid over $5,000 died on the way to this country, suffocated in transit from improper crating. Upon arrival at La Guardia Air Field he was found dead in his crate.

This was not the fault of the shipper who proposed to send the dog in a show basket of wicker with an all-open wire front; but the company removed him from his basket and substituted a solid wooden crate with but sixteen holes along the top of its four sides. To get any air from those high, totally inadequate little openings, the poor dog must have had to stand on his hind legs. The money expended was not lost entirely for the dog was Lloyd insured, but the loss to the breed was great and the tragic circumstances of his suffering and death can never be repaid or forgotten.

Shipping dogs by air in those days was true pioneering, neither the buyer nor the seller knowing what was going to happen, and the transport company with the facilities available acting in all sincerity for the best. Had the new present-day crates been available, that famous little dog would have reached his new home in safety.

There are now available many good crates designed especially for air travel; they are strong but light in weight.

It is easy to understand why dogs travelling by air were formerly restricted to cargo planes only. The new flight kennels, however, now make it possible to transport dogs by passenger planes, which is a big step toward promoting the comfort of the animals as well as the ease of mind for those who wish to take their dogs right along with them on the same plane. Furthermore, shipments will now be accepted for air travel in conjunction with Railway Express if the point of departure is not one of their airports, meaning that a breeder situated at some distance from a commercial airfield can ship by rail part of the way then by air to distant points north, south, east or west along their routes.

Meticulous handling of incoming shipments is as vital to the safety of the dog as is the handling of outgoing shipments. Wise is the breeder, large or small, who takes into consideration the possibility of accident and infection when admitting into his premises unknown dogs from outside kennels. Of course, it may be some time before the novice has a stud dog of his own to which females will be sent for mating. On the other hand, it goes without saying that even during his novitiate he will buy for breeding dogs which may have to be shipped to him. Heartache and disappointment will be avoided if the major phases of the shipping problem are understood.

I am going to discuss the incoming shipment on the basis of the female sent to our kennels for mating, as the methods we have worked out over a period of years I believe will be found equally helpful in the handling of any dog coming from a distance.

If one is conveniently situated the express company will deliver the dog right to the consignee's door. Even when such is the case, valuable time may be lost in awaiting delivery, so our kennelman meets the train or the plane on which the dog is scheduled to arrive. With the express agent he checks the dog's condition; if it arrives with a "blue eye" or filmed eye, or is in any way sick or apparently below par, our man so notes when signing the receipt just in case it may have resulted from negligence and subsequent claim therefore be warranted. We telegraph the owner at once, attempting to minimize possible worry by saying that the dog will be given expert care and kept until the eye is clear or the dog otherwise in fit condition to make the return trip.

We have a large isolation kennel for visiting bitches, with roomy inside pens and hatches opening out into good-sized runways.

Visiting matrons are usually sent to us on tenth day of their season, rested a day or two, then bred when ready and willing to accept the male. They are rested another day or two afterward, then shipped back to the owner in a cleaned crate properly outfitted with water cup, food and feeding directions.

When, for instance, the damaged eye does not clear up in a few days—possibly it has resulted from cold during the incoming trip, or maybe the female has weak eyes requiring special attention—we treat with suitable eye ointments or secure veterinary assistance if we deem it necessary, at the same time again notifying the owner that we will isolate the matron in our kennel until she is well enough to travel.

If the bitch is found to be infested with fleas or lice, she is well dusted with a flea powder; the stud is also protected against infestation by a thorough dusting. We notify the owner regarding the presence of any external parasites on the female, advising that they dip her when she reaches home and keep dipping until the pests are completely eradicated. Until they have experienced just such a siege, few novices realize the extent of trouble caused when the prospective matron is infested because the pests will infest every puppy in the litter.

Upon arrival here, the visiting matron is offered water to drink immediately and allowed to exercise in a secure run. In an hour's time, when the first strangeness will have worn off, she is shut in her pen and a dish containing a good meat mixture left with her. The pen also has a freshly filled water dish, and a sleeping bench or box depending upon the season of year. We cover the floor with newspapers enabling us to note whether she still shows color discharge, also the conditions of urine and bowels. The male is taken to the isolation kennel and the two are bred there.

Despite every precaution, there always remains a certain amount of danger in bringing into one's own kennels, even for a few days, dogs from the outside. The majority of females sent us for breeding come from establishments immaculate and well managed but there is ever that one chance of a matron whose quarters are not kept clean or whose kennel-mates may be infected and, while not infected herself, she may carry germs about with her. This of course is our reason for keeping all incoming shipments isolated.

But, germs being the agile killers they are, we allow for their fence-jumping propensities, as it were, to the extent of asking for definite data on all visiting bitches at the time the first inquiry for service is received. The sum total of this data benefits the bitch and her owner no less than our entire menage. We stipulate that the bitch must have been given permanent inoculation against distemper unless she has recovered from natural distemper which would render her immune thereafter. Otherwise we request that she be given temporary serum before being shipped.

A number of other questions we ask also for the sake of the female's own safety and in order to guide us in the right selection of the stud. Information includes facts regarding registration, age, weight and pedigree.

Age and weight we stress, preferring the second season for an initial mating so the female will be sufficiently developed and sturdy to withstand the ordeal of whelping, while size is equally important to a successful outcome. Many a novice with a few house pets believes it safe to breed a seven-pound bitch; if they insist on mating one so small, we choose one of our older champions of small size, though we discourage any mating at all in such cases, warning the owners of the probable need for a Caesarean.

Usually the beginner's first letter of inquiry as to breeding terms and service dates requests our advice as to selection of the stud. If the pedigree is submitted for our inspection several weeks in advance, after careful study, we inform the owner which dog we think should be used, but we ask the privilege of substituting a second or third choice in the event the first-choice agreed-upon stud refuses to mate her.

Pekingese are temperamental—if the female is cross, or if she snaps in fright, she loses her appeal apparently, when the stud sometimes turns away in unconcern, and there is nothing we can do about it. This is one of the reasons, among many, why we like to see the prospective matron before committing ourselves regarding stud selection. We can note not alone her size but her build, gauge her temperament after a fashion, and point by point check her faults and her virtues. It is a waste of time and money to breed two dogs with like faults, however slight those faults and however illustrious either parent may be. If the bitch represents line breeding or is suitable for inbreeding with our champions we often breed for choice of litter or for one-half the stud fee and second choice puppy.

When after sufficient rest following the mating, the bitch is ready to be returned, we wire the owner the time of departure and probable time of arrival. Then we feed her a big meat meal an hour or two before she is scheduled to leave, turning her out for a good run and making sure she has had a satisfactory bowel movement. We check her condition throughout, clean her eyes, give her a final grooming and drive her to the train or airport. As her papers and contracts have already been made out and have only to be checked by the agent, there is no long wait; off she goes in good spirits and prime condition.

Ch. Yu Sen Yu Toi with Miss Sally Higgs at airport, just before the fatal trip.

Epilogue

Is an Epilogue a Finale? No, I don't believe anything is ever really finished, but I do think I solved the problem of line breeding when, through careful study, I produced the Golden Fleece—Jai Son's perfectly square head, muzzle as wide as his flat top skull, eyes large, dark and set far apart with nose up between them, open nostrils *not* a "pushed-in" nose under a *too* heavy wrinkle; correctly set ears with long ear leather, pear-shaped body, level back, sound low legs, good bone, wide chest, good ear fringes and coat, not the *all over* coat of some modern winners. Jai Son had a waistline and no faults to hide under his coat. His champion sire, champion grandsire and then Ch. Pierrot gave him many of their best points, but I saw the other ancestor's faults and I bred them *out;* their virtues I bred *in*, thus producing Jai Son.

Will our young new breeders take time to do that, to find out the faults back of their dogs, or will they breed, "hit or miss" to the popular winner of the day, trying to get coats instead of trying for type. We all want a nice coat, *but* type comes first. Hit and miss breeding may work once, but that gets you nowhere. In the long run, line breeding and knowing the faults as well as the good points back of sire and dam will eventually produce winners for you.

To crowd into one volume a lifetime of Pekingese is difficult indeed, so much has to be left out. I hope my review of older kennels is not boring to new breeders. Most of their winning dogs go back

Ch. Jai Son Fu was featured in *Life* magazine after his fourth Best in Show win at the Pekingese Club Specialty show. The famous animal photographer, Camilla Koffler, better known as Ylla, came to Orchard Hill and took pictures of Jai Son for the article. Ylla was killed a few years later while on a safari filming wild animals in India.

to our past "greats" and the quality seen in the show ring today proves what yeoman service those pioneers gave us. The Golden Fleece is back now in mythology, but "hope springs eternal" and maybe *You* are the one who will not have to journey to Mount Olympus to find it.

I end with an old Sanskrit saying, "The only thing these dead hands can hold are the things they have given away."

Orchard Hill from the air. Note kennel buildings in the orchard.

Pekingese Breeder Directory

The list which follows is in the nature of a get-acquainted directory which I hope will serve to introduce my host of friends to each other. A lifetime of close association with Pekingese breeders from Maine to California and even far across the seas has taught me that each one of us is needed to assist the other at some time. Both the experienced breeder and the novice oftentimes need help in selecting puppies, in purchasing breeding stock as well as stud services, and they want to find fellow fanciers nearby or perhaps in some particular locality. For this reason I have arranged this section by states for ready reference.

Alabama

Pa We Ja, Mr. & Mrs. Paul Ausman, 921-6th Av. W., Birmingham
Horace Wilhoite, P. O. Box 2013, Montgomery
Kai Shan, 3005 Ellis Dr., Montgomery
Hallmark, Mr. & Mrs. Eston Hallmark, Rt. 8, Box 878, Bessemer
Ray Boyd, Rt. 2, Box 336, Huntsville

Alaska

Nancy Ann Nichols, State Hospitality Center, Tok Junction
Mrs. Charles B. Cowell, 4082-9th St., Apt. 8, Ft. Wainwright

Arizona

Mrs. O. J. Stoker, 2638 E. Edgemont, Phoenix
Mr. & Mrs. Garald Oliverson, 735 S. Pima St., Mesa

Mildred Davenport, 13227 N. 27th St. Pl., Phoenix
Mr. & Mrs. Earl Rooks, 4023 E. Osborn Rd., Phoenix

Arkansas

Fayark Kennels, 228 S. Block Av., Fayetteville

California

Cha Ming. Mrs. Charmain Lansdown, 332 N. Rodeo Dr., Beverly Hills
Mar Pat. Mrs. Martha M. Bingham, 1131-22nd St., Manhattan Beach
Ber Gum. Elaine & William Bergum, 439 S. Ashwood Av., Ventura
Mrs. Anna M. Young, 3308 Brady, Anaheim
Langridge. Mrs. Irene Francisco, 2314 Las Palomas Dr., La Habra
Atherstone. George Bindley Davidson, 450 N. Rossmore Ave., Los Angeles
Hazelle Ferguson, 8700 Hollywood Blvd., Hollywood
Sing Lee. Mrs. Adolph Ruschhaupt, 657 E. Garland Av., Fresno
Pekin Palace. Virginia Selstad, 312 Gird, Chino
Chun Chu Fu. Shirley Stone, 7020 Bellaire, N. Hollywood
Mr. & Mrs. Irving Livingston, 4422 Bakman, N. Hollywood
Don Ho. Donna Creley, 2639 Tulare St., Fresno
Pek Well. 8113 E. Phlox St., Downey
Pierrots' Kennels. Neva McMunn, 17820 S. Evelyn Av., Gardena
Edith V. Butler, 11605 Van Owen, N. Hollywood
Essie Love Jones, 3020 N. Earle St., So. San Gabriel
Browns Den. Cora W. Brown, 6211 Rosemead Blvd., Pico Rivera
Mrs. Evelyn Coursey, 3603 Gangel Av., Pico Rivera
Hei Lein. Mrs. Lois Frank, 206 Haven Av., Chico
Seng Kye. Harry and Amy Aldrich, 34 Terrace Dr., Chico
Arje Wa, Jeannette Watts, 5628 Nona Way, Sacramento
Mrs. Betsy Frey, 509 El Pintado Rd., Danville
Kings Court, James L. King, 4212 Henning Ct., Concord
Doton's, 3082 N. Lima St., Burbank
Alza, 1301 Cameron, Long Beach
San Ri Cam, 655 W. Harvard, Santa Paula
Mrs. Alha E. Walker, 655 W. Howard, Santa Paula
Merritt Olds & David Bevers, 230 Family Farm, R.D., Woodside
Everglo's 1717 Clark Av., Bakersfield

Colorado

Mrs. Charles Binns, 604 Pear St., Pueblo
M. R. Shannon, 3001 Umatilla, Denver
Yung-Sun, K. E. Foster, Rt. 1, Salida

Connecticut

West Winds, Mrs. Horace Wilson, Olmstead Hill Rd., Wilton
Rosedowns, Mrs. Evelyn Ortega, Hideaway Lane, Norwalk

Dorothy P. Lathrop, Juniper Hill Under Mountain Rd., Falls Village
Pentlands, Mrs. Alex Frank, 164 Danbury Rd., Wilton
Jane Chester, 10 Knowles Av. Ext., Middletown

Delaware

Mrs. Hermine Cleaver, Pene Ader, Baltimore Pike R. D. 2, Newark

Florida

Scheid's Va Lee, Box 321, Rt. 2, Bradenton
Ho Ti, Mrs. C. M. Bateman, 40 Odess Lane, Pensacola
Mrs. Sam Jordan, Jr., 1217 E. Mallory St., Pensacola
Mrs. P. M. McGoldrick, P. O. Box 171, Terra Ceia
Mrs. Dolores Gordon, 7932 N. W. 16th Av., Miami

Georgia

Cha Roca, Mrs. C. W. Austin, 130 Robin Lane, Mariette
Mr. & Mrs. Charles C. Venable, 1235 Gresham Av., S. E., Atlanta 16
Mrs. James Childers, 2800 Jonesboro Rd., S. E., Atlanta
Harps Wee Pekingese, 1802 Howell Mill Rd., N. W., Atlanta
Mrs. H. B. Thacker, 1106 Sherman Av., St. Simons Island
Mrs. Gerald M. Livingston, Dixie Plantation, Quitman

Idaho

Ver Jo, Verda Pretl, Castleford
Castleford Kennels, Rt. 1, Buhl
Florence Taylor, 2121 Targes, Boise

Illinois

Four Winds, Mrs. Robert Jackson, Seneca
Lorings, Mr. & Mrs. Al Lind, 4260 River Rd., Schiller Park
Mrs. Elaine Rigden, Edward B. Jenner, Rt. 1, Box 51, Libertyville
Olive Naomi Nelson, 3029 Crescent Pines, E. Waukegan
R. B. Porter, Stronghurst
Stella's Pet Shop, Rt. 30, Chicago Heights
Mrs. George W. Stimke, 1828 N. 5th St., Springfield
Mrs. Frank Fielding, 1409 N. Sharbona St., Streator

Indiana

Don Dee, George & Maude Drake, 201 Church Lane, Bloomington
Chances R, Mr. & Mrs. Marion Chance, 5213 Sadlier Dr., Indianapolis
Mogene, Mr. & Mrs. Benton Dudgeon, Rt. 6, Box 123, Terre Haute
Lusty Wind, Lorraine Heichel, R.R. 2, Box 3, Cedar Lake
Millers Pekingese, Albion

Iowa

Sno Peke, Elk Horn
Wynola, 321 Ridge St., Keokuk
Marjorie Boyington, 113 S. 4th St., Red Oak

Kansas

Rev. & Mrs. Leslie Thomas, Box 321, Bonner Springs

Kentucky

Cho Sen, Mr. & Mrs. G. W. Voyles, 4333 Taylorsville Rd., Louisville
Mrs. Dorothy Gardner, 926 Southview Rd., Louisville
Bey Li, Nell Bailey, White Plains
Mrs. Ralph O'Daniel, Calhoun Rd., Owensboro
Mrs. Al James, 2535 Allen, Owensboro
Mrs. Morrison Kavanaugh, R. 4, Frankfort
Ida Lee Wheeler, Catnip Hill Rd., Nicholasville
Alice L. Ruble, 2715 Lindsey Dr., Hopkinsville
Mitchlee Pekes, Barbourville

Louisiana

Ling Kennels, Earl A. Jorden, 2670 Slidell Av., Slidell

Maine

Elwin W. Bennett, P. O. Box 313, Bucksport
Sylvia W. Vance, 552 Bridgton Rd., Westbrook

Maryland

Mr. & Mrs. Ronald Downey, Rt. 5, Box 778, Cumberland
Mrs. Gaston Remy, 5320 Dogwood Rd., Baltimore
Mrs. Betty Fanning, Rt. #1, Box 16A, Laurel
Virginia L. Barbour, Rt. 1, Box 151, Glendale
Dragon Hai, Fraser & Williams, 8607 Glenn Dale Rd., Lanham
Springbrook, Rt. 1, Box 118, Germantown

Massachusetts

Dah Lyn, John B. Royce, 140 Naples Rd., Brookline
Coronation, Marilyn Allen, 424 S. Main St., Randolph
Esther M. Martin, 35 Lynnfells Parkway, Saugus
Imperial Kennels, 465 N. Main St., Randolph
Leonard W. Carey, Box 44, Main St., Southampton

Dan Mehl, 42 Sheridan St., Haverhill
Cedarwood Pekes, Emily J. Hennessey, 454 Washington, Hanson
Haven Peke Inn, Marion Haven, 25 Shore Drive, Auburn
Tow Kai, Pauline Towk, 14 Lamont St., Pinehurst
Albert Eastman, Pepperell

Michigan

Golden Gay, Adele & Marilyn Butkus, 12095 Cherrylawn, Detroit
Triple Star, Doris O'Daniel, 28148 Powders Rd., Inkster
Mrs. Agnes Dean, 4420 Shubert Av., Flint 7
Fred & Anna Engstrom, 1011 Allison N.W., Grand Rapids
Pekeholme, Mrs. Muriel Freyman, 30 Elm St., Grand Rapids
Mrs. Robert Adams, 3721 Phillips, Kalamazoo
Adam Kennell, 300 N. Webster Av., Greenville
Hamilton's O'dell, 211 Wall St., Kalamazoo
Green River, R. 2 Mancelona
La Dore, P. O. Box 475, Grand Haven
Flora Lu, 3557 Peck St., Grandville

Minnesota

Mrs. C. Atkins, 13 Norman Ridge Rd., Minneapolis
Vincent Lorenzen, 1023 Bush Av., St. Paul
Oka Min, Mr. & Mrs. George Kottke, 1307-7th Av., S. Anoka
Bonnie O. Scholl, Winnebago

Missouri

Kem Haven, Mrs. Glenn Kemper, Route 6, Columbia
Runzi's, R. R. #2, Festus
Mrs. James E. Hankins, 2211 E. Langston, Springfield

Montana

Absar Okee, Mrs. Walter Brant, 319 N. 23rd St., Billings
Wegner, 2059 Washington, Billings
Mrs. Charles F. Jensen, Box 48, 97 A.R.S., Malmstrom A.F.B.

Nebraska

Orpha Jaquish, 2335 "A" St., Lincoln
Mrs. Everett Wright, Chappell
Lester Smith, 4826 S. 47th St., Omaha
Oakhill, C. & S. Fitzpatrick, 8101 N. 44th St., Omaha
Juanita Mueller, Platte Center
Helen Johnson, Crete
Del Rays, Mrs. Peggy Edwards, Box 148, Ulysses

New Hampshire

Pearl Emmons, 31 Temple St., Nashua

New Jersey

Mr. & Mrs. Richard Bell, 721 Kinderkamack Rd., Oradell
Xanadu, Mr. & Mrs. Wheeler Beckett, 277 Walnut St., Englewood
Mrs. James Binaco, 712 Raymere Av., Interlaken
Agnes Stack, 1075 Milton Av., Box 13, Westville
Mrs. Gilma B. Moss, 23 Sutton Dr., Hohokus
Mrs. Dorothy Van Emburgh, 70 Mountain Av., Pompton Plains
Mrs. Florence Gwynne, Box 71, R.R. #1, Vincentown
Allen Stetson, Mt. Laurel Rd., R.D. #2, Mt. Holly

New Mexico

Peke A Toi, Mr. & Mrs. Sam Magun, 10230-4th St., N.W., Albuquerque

New York

Millrose, Mrs. Edwin Blamey, 17 W. 71st St.
Frank Jones, 217 E. 12th St.
David Crawford, 54 W. 16th St.
Palace Guard, William Blair & Lewis Prince, 210 E. 68th St.
Miralac, Mrs. Lillian Clark, Horseshoe Hill, Poundridge
Mrs. Dorothy Dwyer Hanson, Mt. Sinai, L.I.
Peke Haven, Mrs. Frank Hess, 86 La Rue Dr., Huntington, L.I.
Del Vila, Mrs. Justin Herold & Miss Delphine McEntyre, 271 Mamaroneck Rd., Scarsdale
Mr. & Mrs. Roderick Nourse, 90 Siwanoy Blvd., Eastchester
Mrs. Eric Lagercrantz, Ogden Park, Dobbs Ferry
Eaves, C. Houghton, Hacklebarney Cr., 473 Mendon Ionia Rd., Honeoye Falls
Robwood, Mrs. Mary Brewster, Pine Plains
Mrs. Arthur B. Gowie, 902-8th Av., Troy
Star Keys, 4782 Tonawanda Creek Rd., N. Tonawanda
Mrs. Myrtle Raczenski, 4 Quarry St., Phelps
Mrs. Mary E. Spicer, 64 Heberton Rd., Rochester
Mrs. Martha Smith, 24 Tattersall Lane, Albany

North Carolina

Mr. & Mrs. Charles Jordan, 1614 Princeton Av., Charlotte
Newmont, Hauser Rd., Rt. 1, Lewisville
Don Johnson, Route 6, Box 568, Charlotte
Sprinkles, 2387 E. Sprague St., Winston Salem
Goldpytte, Nebo
Joe Worley, Waynesville, Route 3

Ohio

El Acre, Mrs. Vivian Longacre, 4805 Manchester Rd., Akron
Ir Ma Mi, Mrs. Irene Miles, 67 Ridge Rd., Mansfield
Audrianne, Audrey A. Atherton, 7686 Manor Dr., Mentor on the Lake
Presleen, Charleen Prescott, Old Mill Rd., Gates Mills
Goodnor, Burton Andrew & Frank Pietrocini, 2029 Goodnor Rd., Cleveland Heights
Lov Li, Catherine Hendershot, 886 S. State St., Painesville
Popas, Mr. & Mrs. Theodore Popa, 12115 State Rd., R. R. 3, Alliance
Pepekeo, Laura Handley, 1344 S. Main St., Bellefontaine
Mr. & Mrs. Charles Richards, R. D. 1, Bellair
Ruth Berki, 17 W. Vine St., Fairborn
Mie-Har's, M. E. Bufwack-H. Rupert, 1514 Kearney Av., Miles
Eve Ron's, Mr. & Mrs. Ronald Schaefer, Box 11, R. D. 4, Cortland
Char Mai, C. Kniceley, R. D. 2, Greenwich
Mrs. Ralph Snyder, R. R. 1, L & M Motel, Greenville
Mrs. Evelyn Schaefer, Box 11, R. D. 4, Cortland
Elpam, James D. Maple, Box 191, Bergholz
Miss Kitty Duff, 18 Poplar Av., Brookside, Bridgeport
Le Fu's, P. O. Box 117, Vandalia
McBride, Box 223, St. Johns
Ruth Smith, Rt. 2, Republic
Mrs. Herbert Williams, R. R. 2, Bellefontaine
Mr. & Mrs. Lowell Nagel, 427 Woodlawn Av., Bucyrus
Mrs. Harry Gimbel, Route 4, Mansfield
Rinaka, Richard Karn, 3216 Clark State Rd., Gahanna

Oklahoma

Silvanite, Tom & Edna Harper, Rt. 1, Box 76, Tuskahoma

Oregon

Larry W. Anderson, 1048 N. 1st St., Springfield
Rose Marie Jensen, High Valley Farms, Medord

Pennsylvania

Majara, Mrs. Dixon M. Lathrop, R. D. 1, Chester Springs
Mrs. Laure Mosheim, 782 N. Evans St., Pottstown
Bailcliff, Mrs. Ethel Bailie Hillcrest, Doylestown
Highland, Mrs. Elizabeth Delks, Box 84, Point Pleasant, Bucks
Mrs. Mathew Imrie, Lahaska, Bucks
Pickering Forge, Mr. & Mrs. William Gordon, R. D. 2, Charlestown Village, Phoenixville
Valrose, Ralph E. Clevenstine, 57 Ridge Av., Westwood, Coatesville
Candy Sharon Ward, 1013 Ash St., Scranton
Mr. & Mrs. Robert Zettle, Box 257, Houserville Rd., State College
Vesta Lee, R. R. 3, The Poplars, Greenville
Ra Ene, Mr. & Mrs. Raymond Smith, R. D. 7, Station Rd., Erie
Orchard Hill Kennels, Mrs. Richard S. Quigley, Lock Haven

South Carolina

Mrs. W. L. Pittman, Box 248, Rt. 1, Travelers Rest

South Dakota

Bertha L. Worl, 429 East Omaha St., Rapid City

Tennessee

Houston & Peggy Carr, 2077 Whitney Av., Nashville
John L. Morrell, 140 Kingsley Av., Kingsport
Dr. Albert S. Easley, "Windswept," 546 McCallie Av., Chattanooga

Texas

Tien Hia, Mrs. Murray Brooks, 100 Sequois, San Antonio
Quilkin, Mrs. Alice B. Holmes, 12011 Surrey Lane, Houston
He Lo, Mrs. Rubye Turner Williams, 160 Reinecke St., Houston
Mar Chin, Mary McEachin, 2101 Margaret Dr., Houston
Edith Moorehead, 7550 Ashburn St., Houston
Mr. & Mrs. William Kidd, 5763 Flamingo Dr., Houston
Po Yen, Wanda M. Brown, 7751 Alameda Av., El Paso
Kee Woo, Mrs. Ben Blackwell, 1002 Ross Av., Waco
Se Je, Mr. & Mrs. J. E. Garrison, 2921 N.W. 25th St., Forth Worth
Nell O'Herndon, 1204 Kings Hi-Way, Ft. Worth
Bertie Floyd, 2704 Polk St., Amarillo
Hu Wee, Mrs. Lillian Huey, 409 Crockett Dr., Killeen

Utah

Snow Pekes, Mr. & Mrs. L. D. Turner, 3229 N. 400 West, Ogden

Virginia

Bettina Belmont Ward, Middleburg
Mr. & Mrs. Lewis E. Wilkes, 803 Grove St., Bedford
W. Russell Johnson, 111 N. Allen Av., Richmond
Mrs. Dorothy Kay, 2315 Dumbatton Rd., Richmond
Och-K-Ma, Harrup and Allen, Rt. 2, Box 157, Mechanicsville
Mrs. Aline Worke, 3014 Grandy Av., Norfolk
Patricia Vincent, 33 Fiske St., Portsmouth
Leda Nowill, Lunenburg

Washington

Marglo, Grace Krieger, 16508 Hwy. 99, Lynnwood
Han Lin, Mr. & Mrs. Gene Hahnlin, R. 2, Woodinville, Box 2315
Mrs. Ruth Cooksey, 17119-44th St., W., Alderwood Manor

Jalna, Zara Smith and Anne Samek, 10912 Whitman Av., N. Seattle
Rose Wilmosth, 1812 M 190th St., Seattle
Mrs. Charlotte Cowell, 4082-9th St., Apt. 8, A.P.O. #731
Mrs. F. R. McCann, North 4726 Cook St., Spokane
Marvel Runkel, 3333 E. 16th St., Spokane
Ra Lyn, Mrs. Ralph Lynch, North 705 Madison, Spokane
Pan Zee, Lloyd Stacy, P. O. Box 1658, Tacoma

West Virginia

Mrs. Russell Inge, Box 627, 113 E. Concord St., Athens
Lu Chow Pekes, Epling & Russell, 1102 Rosalie St., Charleston
Mr. & Mrs. Raymond Smallwood, Box 301, Rt. 1, Summerville
Peke Land, Mrs. Ronald Randolph, P. O. Box 166, Ripley

Wisconsin

Lema Tom Farms, Mrs. M. J. Thomas, 4116 Monona Dr., Madison

Canada

Mrs. Yan Paul, 709 Shepperd Av., East Willowdale, Ont.
Mr. & Mrs. R. W. Chalton, R. R. 3, St. Thomas, Ont.
Mr. & Mrs. F. Hueston, 94 Arthur Av., Peterborough, Ont.
Mrs. M. V. Mosley, R. R. 1, Whitby, Ont.
Mrs. H. Harris McCleary, R. R. 1, Pickering, Ont.
Jean Grant, "Blossomlea," 97 Yongehurst Rd., Richmond Hill, Ont.
Mrs. C. de P. Doniphan, 3763 Draper Av., Montreal
Mary L. Yoell, 212 N. Marks St., Fort William, Ont.
Cedar Crest, Box 183, Kentville, Nova Scotia
Carita Grieve, Saanighton P. O. B. C.

England

Alderbourne, The Misses Ashton Cross, The Wilderness, Ascot, Berks
Caversham, Miss Mary de Pledge, Beacon View Cottage, Salisbury Rd., Shaftesbury, Dorset
Kyratown, Hindley Taylor, Mossfield Rd., Farnworth, NR. Bolton, Lancs
Wanstrow, Mrs. Donald Wilson, Marston House NR. Frome, Somt.
Ifield, Mrs. Ray Chandler, Worth Cottage Pound Hill, Crawley, Sussex
Chyanchy, Mrs. L. Sawyer, 37 Kings Rd., Uxbridge, Middlesex
Mrs. Marian Birks, Brampton House, Old Hall Rd., Chesterfield
Perryacre, Mrs. Alliston Rae, Fringe Green, Bromsgrove, Worcs.
Mrs. Lyall Collins Pebblecot, Box Hill Rd., Tadeworth, Surrey
Sungay, Mr. & Mrs. R. Jones Oakdean, Twycross Nr. Atherstone, Warwickshire
Blanton, Mary Whitelaw, 46 Willifield Way N.W., London NW 11
Copplestone, Mrs. Bentinck Sparks Farm, Barkham Nr. Wokingham, Berks
Coughton, Lady Isabel Throckmortons Coughton, Alcester
Helenes, Mrs. Helena Chester, Clermont Rd., Preston Park, Brighton

Tri-Int. Ch. Pierrot of Hartlebury, from painting by Mrs. Herbert Mapes.

Eloc, Mrs. Lucy Cole, 109 Sunnyhill Rd., Streatham, London
Silverdjinn, Mrs. N. McFarlane, 30 Snaresbrook Dr., Stanmore, Middlesex
Chin Toi, Miss Page, 16 Areindel Gardens, Goodmayes Ilford, Essex
Jamestown, Mrs. Eisenman, Mayfield Colehill, Wimborne, Dorset
Goofus, Roberta Ogle Grasslands, Horsell Common, Woking, Surrey
Mrs. Pownall Grove Lodge Colchester, Essex
Drakehurst, Mrs. L. R. Drake, 1 Exetor Rd., Braunton, Devon
Kin Wong, Mrs. G. A. G. Williams, Hatfield House, Bath, Somerset
Yu Sen, Miss Sally Higgs 1471 Stratford Rd., Hall Green, Birmingham
Wongville, Miss M. Hilton 10 Alexandra Rd., Weymouth, Dorset

Other Countries

Patricia McDonall, 27 Ponsonby Parade Seaforth N.S.W., Australia
Mrs. V. M. Siebert, c/o P. O. Box 16, Bulawayo, Southern Rhodesia
Marchesa Maria Luisa Bourbon del Monte, "La Garnasca" Bellagio, Lake Como, Italy

THE ENDS

Dot
& Fortune
Warren

56 Florence
Green Ridge, Pa.
TR6-9426

Debbie O.

LE2-3818